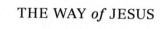

THE WAY *of* JESUS

THE WAY
of JESUS

*Living a Spiritual
and Ethical Life*

JAY PARINI

Beacon Press
Boston

Beacon Press
Boston, Massachusetts
www.beacon.org

Beacon Press books
are published under the auspices of
the Unitarian Universalist Association of Congregations.

21 20 19 18   8 7 6 5 4 3 2 1

This book is printed on acid-free paper that meets the uncoated paper
ANSI/NISO specifications for permanence as revised in 1992.

Text design and composition by Michael Starkman
at Wilsted & Taylor Publishing Services

Library of Congress Cataloging-in-Publication Data

Names: Parini, Jay, author.
Title: The way of Jesus : living a spiritual and ethical life / Jay Parini.
Description: Boston : Beacon Press, 2018. | Includes bibliographical
    references.
Identifiers: LCCN 2017030573 (print) | LCCN 2017058132 (ebook) | ISBN
    9780807047255 (e-book) | ISBN 9780807047248 (hardcover : alk. paper)
Subjects: LCSH: Jesus Christ—Example. | Christian life.
Classification: LCC BT304.2 (ebook) | LCC BT304.2 .P37 2018 (print) | DDC
    230—dc23
LC record available at https://lccn.loc.gov/2017030573

For Devon,

  who has walked

    beside me

      on the Way

CONTENTS

Preface   ix

ONE: Journeying by Faith   1

TWO: The Christian Mind   34

THREE: The Church Year   109

FOUR: How to Be a Christian   146

Conclusion   184

Acknowledgments   189

Notes   191

Index   195

This book follows from an earlier one, *Jesus: The Human Face of God* (2013). There I looked briefly at the life of Christ, arguing that his story represents a kind of *mythos*, the Greek word for "myth," which I defined not as a story that is untrue but as one that is especially true. What interested me were the symbolic contours of his life, his example of suffering and rebirth, and his remarkable teachings, which have been hugely influential. They have changed the lives of billions of people over two millennia, including my own.

In this study I examine what it means to follow the Way of Jesus, his path toward God, and his effort to seek out and create the Kingdom of God, as defined by himself and some of his most effective and influential interpreters, such as Paul—the great apostle—and generations of writers and thinkers who have confronted his teachings and example, all of them attempting to put them into practice. I begin with a chapter on my own spiritual progress over the past six (nearly seven!) decades, a wandering path in and out of Christianity, during which times I've embraced many versions of what it means to trust in God and follow the example of Jesus. In the subsequent chapters, I frequently allude to my own struggles and occasional successes, dealing frankly with my occasionally vexed relations with traditional ideas about salvation, which I prefer to call "enlightenment," a better translation of the Greek term *soteria*.

In the second chapter, I examine the Christian mind, its complexities, and the problems that Christian thinking attempts to solve or understand. I take it for granted that most people these days, especially well-educated ones, have little time for supernatural religion or religious practices. I address some key philosophical issues frankly, stepping into the areas of epistemology and ontology: these, in turn, refer to the theory of knowledge and ideas about existence itself, and how we come to be who we are. As I must, I draw on a range of ancient and modern theologians, poets, and thinkers, quoting freely throughout. My own thinking operates within a web of textuality, and I try to acknowledge that freely, as a way of marking my own debts but also as a way of directing readers to other useful texts. In this chapter I look closely at the biblical tradition, including the Hebrew and Greek scriptures, and point in other directions as well, including the Gnostic Gospels. In other parts, I confront various matters of concern to Christians, including the stumbling blocks of miracles (and the supernatural) and human suffering. This chapter ends with a reading of the Resurrection as something more than simple resuscitation. It's about ongoing change, the daily rebirth and renewal of the spirit.

In the third chapter I turn to the nitty-gritty of Christian practice, as represented by the Church Year. Christians have been given a huge gift, the cycle of the seasons, with liturgical markers throughout. Christmas and Easter are simply the high points of this complex cycle. The calendar works to further our trust in God, to deepen our sense of what it means to follow the Way of Jesus. It also serves to bring the faith community into focus, into reality. Public prayer and confession and Holy Communion remain vital aspects of any Christian life, and I do my best to outline the course of this unfolding calendar, with its unique liturgies and language, its profusion of symbols, its manner of lifting us over and through the days of the year as we follow in the steps of Jesus.

In the final main chapter, I use T. S. Eliot's classic collection of poems *Four Quartets* as a guide to Christian living. These four poems, which are in each case a sequence of connected poems, draw heavily on the language of Christianity while bringing into play insights from Hinduism and Buddhism as well. Eliot was a remarkable man, and his profound thinking about the work of the spirit in the life of the active mind is for me exemplary, infinitely suggestive. In the third sequence, "The Dry Salvages," Eliot marks out five key things for Christians to consider as they follow the Way of Jesus: "Prayer, observance, discipline, thought, and action." I consider each of these in turn, with personal reflections on their importance as signposts along the Way. Eliot's sense of eternity as "here, now, always" strikes me as a perfect description of salvation. His approach, in its modesty and profundity, remains part of my life, and I reread this sequence of poems often.

This isn't a work of evangelism. It's an attempt to understand what Jesus really meant, his effort to put love first and foremost in our daily lives, and to describe my own efforts to follow his example. My hope is that this book will prove helpful to others who struggle, as I do, with some of the basic questions about human existence: its limits and sadness, its possibilities for awareness and understanding, its undeniable glories, believing firmly that in Jesus, "all things are possible" (Mark 10:27).

THE WAY *of* JESUS

ONE

JOURNEYING BY FAITH

> The eye is the first circle; the horizon which it forms is the second; and throughout nature this primary figure is repeated without end. It is the highest emblem in the cipher of the world. Saint Augustine described the nature of God as a circle whose center was everywhere, and its circumference nowhere. We are all our lifetime reading the copious sense of this first of forms.
> —*Ralph Waldo Emerson, "Circles"*

I often think of my own faith journey—or journeys—as a zigzag path over many decades, with numerous periods of drought, stretches of complete indifference and alienation from God, when I felt the brown cracked earth under my feet. The journey was never easy, and it remains just as tortuous after many decades, although it helps to have some experience with spiritual trekking itself. Of course, there were exhilarating times at every point, oases of connection, with a sense of being part and parcel of a larger spirit that holds me, and everyone, in loving embrace. These are the times Saint Paul refers to in 1 Corinthians 15:28, occasions when we sink into the experience of unity with God (atonement) deeply and completely, "until God becomes all in all." This is salvation, that healing motion of the soul, and the destination we seek.

I remember so vividly reading in Emerson's journals as a young man. He wrote that the "highest revelation is that God is in every man," and I underlined this passage several times, with exclamation marks in the margins. Yes, I thought: God is here, inside me, inside everyone. He is the center of the endless circles we trace throughout our lives. Only recently, in fact, a friend asked me where I thought God was, and I touched the coffee table before us, and I said, "In this wood." And it seemed astonishingly true.

I wish I could say that the times of connection or atonement (meaning at-one-ment with God), with their exhilaration and peace, were common occurrences in my life. But they remain moments in and out of time, experienced less often in church or periods of focused devotion than on country roads in late summer, in the leafy woods near my house, sitting by a pond, reading in bed, or writing in a café. Quite often they have been found in conversations with my wife, who has followed her own intense path toward God, often coinciding with mine, over nearly four decades. She and I have shared a great deal on so many levels.

My particular journey of faith—I prefer the word "trust," a better translation of the Greek word *pistis*—began in Scranton, Pennsylvania, where I grew up in the fifties and early sixties in a small house on South Rebecca Avenue: a neighborhood that had been populated over the decades by Welsh, Irish, Italian, and a variety of Eastern European immigrants drawn by the anthracite mining industry, which had rapidly shrunk in the postwar years as the mines emptied of coal. The traces of this industry could be found in the abandoned breakers and burning culm dumps that scarred the landscape, in the dangerously unsupported shafts that webbed beneath the ground and made for any number of accidents. Dozens of churches could be found in most neighborhoods, from Welsh Baptist to Roman Catholic, with an assortment of Orthodox churches, from Lithuanian to Ukrainian and Polish. I remember asking my father why there were so many churches, and he said, "God can't make up his mind where to land."

That was true in his case. He had been raised a Roman Catholic, and my paternal grandmother was devout in the way of Italian immigrants of her era, questioning very little, respectful of the local priests and nuns, vaguely dedicated to the saints and holy days. I felt close to her, and remember seeing a rosary by her bed table. I asked about it, and she explained to me about its use in devotions. She urged me to take up the practice myself, although she knew I attended a Baptist church. A portrait of the Virgin Mary with her child in her arms hung above my grandmother's bed, with a number of pale straws from Palm Sundays past strung through the wire that held the picture in place. Religion was a habit of hers, taken for granted ever since her childhood in a small village near the sea, just south of Venice. My paternal grandfather, on the other hand, showed no interest in religion whatsoever, being a naturally secular man who had abandoned his family early in my father's life. "He's not important to me," my father said, with some bitterness.

My mother's family was from English stock on both sides (with a few Jewish ancestors on the family tree), and her mother was a Baptist, a devotee of the "old-time religion" and with no formal education. Her husband, like my other grandfather, was irreligious, though he was dragged into church on Christmas and Easter. He tolerated my grandmother's obsession with the church, which had become the focal point of her life, almost a substitute for family. My own mother was a Baptist by tradition, moderately devout at various times in her life, with no inclination to question her faith. I recall pointing out to her once (in a fit of youthful arrogance) that her beloved King James Version of the Bible was simply a translation from the Hebrew and Greek scriptures, to which she replied: "If it was good enough for Jesus, it's good enough for me."

I grew up in my mother's home church and was fully immersed at twelve in a warm tub of water behind the pulpit. I recall services at the Jackson Street Baptist Church with a kindly old man at the helm, the Reverend Bair. The long, hot summer services with teeming crowds of believers shouting "Amen" at notable points in the sermon stay in my mind. The evangelical aura of this church shifted when a bright young man named Bill Lewis was called to the pulpit after Bair died. He became a friend, and I found myself (in early adolescence) awakened to religious questions. Was the Bible the inerrant and infallible word of God? Did everyone go to hell who didn't "believe in the Lord Jesus?" I remained troubled by such questions throughout high school, but the piping hymns lodged in my brain, and I came to like the texture of the services, with their ringing hymns and emotional sermons. I often still sing a few of my favorite Baptist hymns in the car when I'm driving alone.

The quality of my early experience of the church shifted when my father, in his late thirties, became a fierce born-again Christian. I happen to know the exact date of this, as I inherited his old Bible and he had written on the first page: "I was saved on August 16, 1954, by the grace of God." He had been taken by a friend to a Billy Graham revival meeting and was utterly transformed by this experience. In his mind, Jesus became his personal savior—a late-breaking version of Paul on the Road to Damascus. A profound transformation occurred. He soon began to study the Bible passionately and attended weekly prayer meetings. He joined a group of local businessmen who shared his passion for religion, and they would meet for discussion and lunches at least once a month. Every morning before the rest of the family awakened he would descend into the living room, where he read and prayed for an hour. In a few years he joined a Bible school in the evenings, and he eventually became ordained as a Baptist preacher. (To be frank, he had no gift for preaching, although he communicated a certain godly presence in the pulpit, which his parishioners admired. And he modeled the gentleness of behavior that Saint Paul urged upon all Christians.)

My father wasn't especially communicative, at least not with me, and I've long wondered about the origins of his radical conversion. Was he running away from something? I've no doubt his rough childhood in an Italian family had sketchy episodes, yet he always seemed by nature a good-hearted fellow, low-key, rarely prone to excess of any kind. It was not, for him, a big sacrifice when he gave up alcoholic beverages and curse words. Nevertheless, he pursued his new faith with unmistakable consistency and focus, intent upon saving souls whenever he could. Indeed, at one point he would put little stickers on the mirror in the bathroom to count "souls" that he had saved. He carried a packet of religious tracts in his briefcase as well as miniature copies of John's Gospel, and it didn't take much for him to give one or both of these away.

I would cringe when he would say to an absolute stranger: "Do you, by any chance, know Jesus?"

His religious studies consumed him, and I would say good night to him in the kitchen as he pored over the Bible and related books, which he filled with marginalia. His old King James Bible in the odd but wildly influential Scofield edition rests on my desk, and I often dip into it just to read his comments. They are strikingly sincere, intelligent, thoughtful, as when he underscores a verse from Ezekiel 33:11: "As I live, saith the Lord God, I have no pleasure in the death of the wicked; but that the wicked turn from his way and live." In the margins he wrote, "This shows God's graciousness. How wonderful!" He listened every Sunday at lunchtime to Billy Graham on the radio, as did the whole family.

My father would read the Bible aloud each morning at the breakfast table to my sister and me. I listened closely, alert to the seductive rhythms and imagery on parade. The archetypical stories and eloquent proverbs stuck with me. Encouraged by him, we memorized verses to recite before bedtime, and to this day I have a fair portion of the Bible in my head. My own allegiance to poetry—a lifelong habit of reading and writing—dates to those days, and to my visceral response to the rhythms of the King James translation of 1611. How could you not respond to passages like this one, from Ecclesiastes?

> I returned, and saw under the sun, that the race is not to the swift, nor the battle to the strong, neither yet bread to the wise, nor yet riches to men of understanding, nor yet favor to men of skill; but time and chance happeneth to them all.

My father especially liked the book of Proverbs, and I can still hear his voice, which carried over the crunching of cereal in my mouth: "My son, if thou wilt receive my words, and hide my commandments with thee; So that thou incline thine ear unto wisdom, and apply thine heart to understanding; Yea, if thou criest after knowledge, and liftest up thy voice for understanding; if thou seekest her as silver, and searchest for her as for hid treasure; then shalt thou understand the fear of the Lord, and find the knowledge of God" (Proverbs 2:1–5). He spent the last five decades of his life seeking after this knowledge, and I'd like to believe he found it.

I can't say that I simply accepted the truth of Christianity in its Baptist inflections, as they seemed to me literal-minded, even self-satisfied. There was a tone of rebuke in many of the sermons I heard that struck me then as thoroughly against the grain of Jesus's teaching, at least insofar as I could understand it. Too much emphasis was placed on the inerrancy of the Bible, which anyone could see was riddled with inconsistencies and inscrutable passages. I was, as the hymn goes, "almost persuaded"—but never fully persuaded. The fact that other religions existed troubled me. I don't think I was more than nine or ten when it occurred to me that Hindus, Buddhists, Muslims, Jews, and countless others in far-flung regions (or next door) didn't accept Jesus as their personal savior, so they were—in theory—bound for hell. It worried me that my church paid allegiance to a God who could be so vengeful, ignoring the obvious fact on the ground that a lot of people had other ideas about the nature of God or the path to salvation. And many, of course, had no thought about these matters whatsoever.

I remember asking Pastor Lewis about Hindus and Buddhists, and he said with a kind of cramped wisdom, "I suppose they take comfort in their religions as we do in ours." He also said, "God is tolerant, and so we should be ourselves." Needless to say, Bill Lewis went down badly among many in the church, who found his broad-mindedness antithetical to their ideas of proper Christian thinking. But he wakened in me both a tolerance of and a curiosity in other faiths, and this would continue to shape my thinking as I moved into adulthood.

The amount of suffering in the world became another stumbling block to my early faith. How could the God I wanted to trust with a childlike simplicity be so randomly cruel? Was he toying with us? Could he possibly be omnipotent and therefore capable of changing anything while continuing to allow for cruelty? I knew about the Holocaust: it happened only a few years before my birth, and one veteran of the war who attended my church had helped to liberate Auschwitz. He told my Sunday school class about what happened there and I remained in near shock for weeks. Did God simply turn his face from this sort of atrocity? What kind of thing was the human spirit that it could descend to such brutality?

We used to dive under our desks in elementary school, practicing for the nuclear attack that every adult seemed to believe was sure to come. I remember reading about what happened in Hiroshima and Nagasaki, and it occurred to me then that this kind of evil didn't bear thinking about. It was painful to imagine that we, God-fearing Americans all, had unleashed this fury on a civilian population. Had this somehow been part of God's larger plan, as my father explained to me patiently when I asked? Did we not bear some collective responsibility for such a quantum of misery?

In the fifth grade I watched the father of a classmate die of leukemia, and I realized how fragile we were as human beings. We were programmed to die. I saw my own grandmother suffer from severe diabetes, a condition that led to the amputation of her legs when I was eleven, and her intense suffering weighed on me. A neighbor who had been very kind to me (we spent long hours on his porch talking about his experiences in World War II) died suddenly one evening of a heart attack, leaving behind a helplessly bereaved young family with few economic resources. I knew in a gut sense that suffering was central to the human experience. It lay about us everywhere. And I had no chance to escape this misery.

A hypochondriac myself, I worried about illness and death, no doubt excessively. Talk of cancer would freak me out, and I recall being panicked by the death of John Foster Dulles, the secretary of state under President Eisenhower, in 1959. Accounts of his final agonies were widely reported, and they kept me awake at night. If this could happen to someone as prominent as Dulles, what hope was there for me? Of course, I worried that my own father would drop dead, as did so many men in the fifties, before people understood that smoking was bad for you, and before high cholesterol and high blood pressure were solvable problems.

Mortality unnerved me, and I needed relief. Yet I found it difficult to take consolation from an arbitrarily vengeful God who had gone so far as to insist that his own son be crucified because Adam and Eve, a couple on some remote and minor planet called Earth, had chosen to disobey his apparently random rules. It further upset me that we, the godforsaken children of Adam and Eve, had been condemned sight unseen because of something they did such a long time ago. Could Almighty God have been so horribly bent out of shape because Eve had eaten from the forbidden tree? Where was his famous compassion? I didn't like a God who would send a flood to destroy the world, leaving only Noah and his wife to start it anew with their tiny boatload of birds and animals. I hated the way God toyed with Abraham, suggesting that he must kill Isaac, his beloved son—just to test his faithfulness. I couldn't understand the way he tortured poor

Job, just to see if he could make him denounce his creator. There was so much not to like about this God that I struggled with praising him. It seemed hard to "make a joyful noise unto the Lord," as the psalmist urged. He seemed intolerant, willful, and somewhat thin-skinned.

Then again, I saw the benign effects that the practice of religion had on my father, as well as on numerous people in my church. I was also moved by the sermons of any number of excellent preachers. We attended evangelical meetings quite often, and rarely did a bad speaker get to his feet. (I experienced only one female preacher in all my childhood years, and her physical appearance and manner were so unusual—birdlike, wizened, wise—that I recall her name fondly: Miss Elizabeth Williams. In summers I listened to sermons at "tent meetings," as they were called. The evangelists who swept into town for a week or two at a time were masterful rhetoricians, with rolling speech rhythms and riveting stories. They would always make it personal. I admired Billy Graham, too, attending several of his rallies, tuning in to his radio and TV broadcasts. His unambiguous spirituality, charm, and forthright manner appealed to me, and they still do. I understood, in a visceral way, that giving one's heart to Jesus—to God in human form—could be important, although I didn't quite comprehend the mysterious nature of this act or why it seemed to work so well. The whole was a great puzzle.

In high school I spent Monday evenings at the Hyde Park Bible Institute, where I studied the scriptures with a tall, sweaty, bald man with a huge dent in his forehead and a booming voice. He was a graduate of Princeton Theological Seminary, and I liked his keen attention to the texts, which he had absorbed deeply. He was the first genuine scholar I ever encountered and I spent many hours in conversation with him. He urged me not to doubt that God's revelation was thorough and rational, if properly understood. I admired his confident manner, if not his literal readings of scripture, and probably absorbed many of his mannerisms, which included elaborate hand gestures when he grew animated by a particularly striking thought.

In high school I would occasionally attend services of an evangelical group called Youth for Christ, although I found their proselytizing an embarrassment. I went through a period in the tenth grade when I met with other Christian teens in a small church beside my school in West Scranton, although I felt uncomfortable there. We met for roughly an hour before classes started in the often icy pews, reading the Bible aloud, praying, telling one another to "bear witness" in the day ahead. I found the language of this version of Christianity, with its zealotry and literal-mindedness, quite unconvincing, although I kept this to myself. The young evangelical preacher who led this merry band of adolescents seemed full of his own ego. And I didn't think many of these young Christians had enough good sense to question their beliefs in serious ways, as much as I admired their enthusiasm. But I didn't share their passion and I certainly never tried to convert anyone to this brand of faith. My own skeptical nature— it's deeply ingrained, probably an inheritance from my two secular grandfathers—dampened the urge to evangelize, a drive that requires a degree of certainty I could never claim.

Through all of this, I attended church regularly and developed a practice of reading the Bible before sleep, focusing mainly on the psalms and the Gospels. (I really disliked the feverish book of Revelation, which is always a favorite of evangelical preachers, who insist on finding prophesies in certain passages that allude to current geopolitical situations. During the Cold War, the great apocalyptic battle of Armageddon would also involve a clash of American and Soviet tanks.) I occasionally prayed, going through Jesus as the appropriate route to God. And I did, at times, find comfort in these prayers, however irresolute and halfhearted my efforts. It was a kind of meditation, self-centered, as I frequently asked to be spared this or that disease. My prayers were petitions of sorts. I usually put in a good word for my loved ones, too, asking that God spare them from car accidents, cancer, and other catastrophic fates. Once in a while, I prayed that God would give me a car when I turned sixteen. (I'm happy to say he did, in the form of my grandfather's discarded '54 Ford, a deep-throated rust bucket.)

Everything changed when I left home in 1966. I went off to Lafayette College, not far from Scranton in miles but light-years in emotional distance from my childhood. On Sundays I went to services in Hogg Hall, where the chaplain was F. Peter Sabey, a sincere, wonderfully intelligent, and politically charged young man who spoke with great sincerity, a moral edge, and a breadth of religious vision. I had never heard anything like this before, and I began to hang around him, hoping to absorb some of his intellectual shimmer and political passion. His teaching (and preaching) affected me permanently. I found his social activism inspiring and felt drawn to his antiwar sentiments. He convinced me that the war in Vietnam was immoral as well as impractical. It wasn't hard to convince me of this, as I was threatened by the draft, and my reading on the nature and course of this war upset me. Our destructive intervention in Southeast Asia horrified me, and I was moved by critics such as Noam Chomsky and Howard Zinn, among others. In a first step toward my own activism, I joined a large protest at the Pentagon in Washington, DC, in 1967—an event memorably described by Norman Mailer in *The Armies of the Night*. I recall hearing Dr. Benjamin Spock give a sharply worded address at the Lincoln Memorial, and I marched with thousands to the Pentagon itself, where violence broke out when some tried to push through a military barricade. A motley crew of students with long hair and beards chanted to levitate the building, and some saw it rise into the air and turn orange (I was not among them). Hundreds of protesters were arrested, but I stepped away from that, although I did manage to fling a bucket of sheep's blood on a public building. I felt uncertain, however, about the extent that one should push in the direction of civil disobedience and left the scene before the worst of the violence occurred. The whole event did, in fact, steel me against the war, as I began to understand for the first time the ferocity and responsibility of American power.

During my sophomore year in college I attended weekly prayer meetings, led mostly by students. I found this small but sincere group different from anything I'd experienced before. There was an openness to different iterations of faith, with none of the evangelical zealotry I'd associated with prayer meetings. Inspired by one or two friends, I toyed with the idea of a career in the ministry, looking through various catalogues of divinity schools, although I doubted I had a vocation for this work. I had pretty much decided on a career in writing and teaching, and I rarely wavered in this.

Although I majored in history and literature, I took several courses in religion, and these had a transforming effect. I recall reading *The Dynamics of Faith*, by Paul Tillich, which led me to other books by this liberal Protestant theologian who had redefined God as one's "ultimate concern." He describes the Almighty as "the infinite power of being," and I liked the widening of this holy circle. In his *Systematic Theology*, Tillich writes that God "transcends the power of being and also the totality of being—the world."[1] This sounds like atheism or pantheism to many ears, but it's not. As I saw it, Tillich pointed to a reality outside of what we could know, or how we moved in the world. This God was everywhere, and beyond the materiality of what I experience each day: the earth beneath my feet, the walls of buildings, natural objects, other people.

I think I was most disturbed by the idea of God as one's "ultimate concern." Read in a simplistic way, this seemed to suggest that God was whatever you wanted him to be, or whatever obsessed you. Sex might be God. Or nature. Or one's own anxieties about death. Slowly, I reexamined this phrase and began to think of God as being somehow beyond definition—a power at the heart of everything that mattered to me, just out of reach but somehow present: like someone standing, even breathing, behind a closed door.

The word "God" became for me a useful handle for an experience of something difficult to describe, a presence that I felt strongly but could not call out easily or name. In short, Tillich helped me to reconsider God in fresh but uneasy terms. Tillich became an obsession at the time, a kind of friendly if provocative aid who allowed me to apply my reasoning powers in ways that previously I had kept at bay, afraid that somehow I would destroy my faith if I thought too hard about its essentials or persisted in asking problematic questions. I also read with fascination other modern (mostly German) theologians, including Reinhold Niebuhr, Karl Barth, and Rudolf Otto, each of whom opened vistas that I had not quite imagined could exist, with their distinctly different notions of God. (Just the idea that these very smart men could think about God in radically different ways provided some peculiar comfort: perhaps I could find my own definition, and it would have a reality for me that need not translate broadly to the rest of the world.) Otto's classic book titled *The Idea of the Holy* struck me as one of the most profound meditations I had ever encountered on the idea of the "numinous," a realm that glistens with its own realities. Writing in 1917, Otto considered the idea of "the holy" as a category of value: "The consciousness of a 'wholly other' evades precise formulation in words, and we have to employ symbolic phrases which seem sometimes sheer paradox, that is, irrational, not merely non-rational, in import. So with religious awe and reverence."[2]

I soon came to regard poetry as one of the primary means for me to come to terms with this "wholly other" entity, and that has never changed. Often I return to my favorite poets: Whitman and Dickinson, Wordsworth, Frost, Yeats, Eliot, and Stevens. These are just the core, with Emerson—the true father of my thinking—always present in his essays, and with Thoreau as another touchstone. I take, for instance, infinite comfort in Whitman's bold declarations in "Song of Myself," where he writes with his singular, odd freshness about his experience of God's presence in the everyday world:

Why should I wish to see God better than this day?
I see something of God each hour of the twenty-four, and each
    moment then,

In the faces of men and women I see God, and in my own face
  in the glass,
I find letters from God dropt in the street, and every one is
  sign'd by God's name,
And I leave them where they are, for I know that wheresoe'er
  I go,
Others will punctually come for ever and ever.

In college I also read Martin Buber, the Austrian-born Israeli philosopher, for the first time, and with awe. I savored his poetic *I and Thou,* needing to buy several copies as I kept wearing them out with underlining and marginalia. In what Buber describes as the "I-thou" experience, we—as human beings—enter into relationships with the sacred. And in these relations we discover the holy. "All real living is meeting," Buber writes, and it's often in the meeting of others that we encounter God"[3]—a point I would only much later identify with the marvelous teachings of the so-called Desert Fathers, those hermits and mystics who lived in Egypt at the beginning of the third century after Christ. For them, as for Buber, Christ—the mystical savior—could be found only in community, in contact with another person, in personal transactions, in the creation of community itself. They understood that, as much as anything, our life will be found among others, with our neighbors, who make God visible to us. Reading Buber, these ideas about Christ glimmered faintly in the peripheral vision of my intelligence, still cloudy, but I began slowly to understand that "meeting" others, in a complex and deep sense, would prove essential to whatever spiritual understandings would come toward me.

To experience the more orthodox side of theology, I turned to the Swiss theologian Karl Barth. John Updike, one of my favorite writers at the time, had recommended Barth (in one of his reviews) as a guide to Christian thinking, and Barth seemed to me attractive if, at times, a bit austere and forbidding. I struggled with the ways he grappled with the Calvinist idea of "election," wondering how God could ever choose sides with one person against another. Wasn't this a bit ungenerous of God? What I loved about Barth, however, was his emphasis on the absolute freedom of God, who does not need us, who is utterly beyond us. His emphasis on revelation—especially the revelation of the Word of God in scriptures—appealed to me. In his commentary on Paul's letter to the Romans, a many-layered work of scholarship that I encountered in graduate school a few years later, Barth suggests that God's existence "is distinguished qualitatively from men and from everything human, and must never be identified with anything which we name, or experience, or conceive, or worship, as God."[4] I liked being made aware of the absolute "otherness" of God, who is not, like Jesus, our "friend." There is an austerity in the Godhead that we can't, as human beings with notably limited intellects, even begin to comprehend. Somehow Barth spoke to my own feelings of inadequacy, and seemed to pat me on the back, saying, "There, there, child. Don't try so hard."

Barth's emphasis on the revelation of Christ also struck an important note for me. The God that Barth described seemed austere and difficult to know, far removed from human realities. But the appearance of Christ, in the person of Jesus, was God's way of revealing himself to human beings, for whom otherwise he would remain unknowable. Jesus, as the perfection of humanity, showed us what God was really like. And I began to see Jesus, and God as well as revealed in Jesus, as the definition of compassion. Certainly the Gospels reveal a man-god who is infinitely patient, infinitely loving, and who shows us that the complete love of God obliterates all other realities, and heals the brokenness and alienation that mark our condition. In this sense, salvation is, indeed, a healing of the original wound, a move toward health and wholeness. I only wish I had been able, in my midtwenties, to grasp all of this emotionally as well as intellectually; but the truth here remains, even now, difficult to embrace as thoroughly as I would like, requiring that crucial leap of faith one hears so much about.

Rudolf Bultmann held another kind of fascination for me. He shocked me by arguing that one could know little about the historical Jesus or his context, that we should not ask who Jesus "really" was or even "if" he really was. It was the inherent and core message that mattered, the *kerygma*. This kind of talk at first unnerved me. Of course Jesus "was." If he somehow didn't exist, wasn't everything I ever thought about Christianity some kind of nonsense? In many eloquent essays and books Bultmann suggested that Jesus offered a way of thinking about God and his relationship to human beings in mythic terms that demanded endless reinterpretation. Bultmann's lifelong effort to "demythologize" the New Testament arrested my attention. I read in (not completely "through") his erudite *History of the Synoptic Tradition*,[5] where I learned that the Gospels had a complex textual history and could not simply be read as "true" stories. They were not biographies in any conventional sense, nor were they eyewitness accounts by men called Matthew, Mark, Luke, and John. Instead, they were documents constructed from a mix of oral history and earlier texts that were lost in time. Luke and Matthew drew heavily on Mark's Gospel, which drew on some earlier manuscript or manuscripts in circulation among early followers of The Way. The Gospel of John was very late, possibly dating to the second century, and was unlike the three earlier Gospels, containing any number of stories (such as the Wedding at Cana) and sayings of Jesus that were unknown to the other three Gospel writers.

This rush of new knowledge left me dizzy, and I went home to Scranton one weekend and confronted my father with the fruits of my woefully incomplete new "learning." He must have thought: "This wiseass kid thinks he knows a thing or two. Am I really paying for this?" He was patient with me, however, nodding and smiling, offering mild objections, posing questions. I don't think my pseudoscholarly rambles shook his faith even a little, and I'm glad they didn't. He knew a thing or two himself, and I would like to think he understood, in his own way, what Saint Anselm meant when he wrote about faith as a quest for knowledge: "For I do not seek to understand so that I may believe; but I believe so that I may understand."[6]

In the course of several years I spent a lot of time reading various Christian theologians but also studied Eastern religions, which led me to Taoism and the *Tao Te Ching*—still an essential part of my spiritual life. The initial impact of this tradition was profound, adjusting my sense of the world in subtle ways. Taoism is, in fact, a philosophy more than a religion, though I equate the Tao with God, an Eastern version of the creator as the ground of being. I especially admired the Taoist teaching of the *wu wei*: the process of allowing things to run their natural course, never striving. "Do not let go of the Way," we read in the fourteenth segment. "It's an ancient thread that runs back to the source." The Way of the Tao celebrates emptiness and quiet, a stepping away from the little self and its many loud distractions: "The return to the root of all being is silence." The Taoists had an affinity for nature, and they conformed to the natural world, aware that they were a little part of that world, accepting its rhythms, its prerogatives and limitations. This is akin to "thy will be done" in the Lord's Prayer. Taoists keep their focus in the present, the Eternal Now, facing the truth, whatever it might be, and accepting that change is where we live and that nothing lasts forever—and yet, paradoxically, believing that whatever we love remains.

In the thirteenth segment of the *Tao Te Ching*, this wise teaching occurs:

> See the world as yourself.
> Trust in the way things are.
> Love the world as yourself as well:
> then you can treasure all things.

Such lovely teachings blur the ordinary dualities that plague us: body and soul, self and other, subject and object. Contrarieties, even stark dualisms, may be useful but they are, like so much else, in themselves mental constructions, containing less truth value than we might imagine. Taoism invites us to consider the world as ourselves, inside and out. It asks us not to worry about the world's opinion, to let that go, finding in ourselves a way to adjust our pace and posture to accommodate the rhythms of the world. There is nothing but freedom in the Tao, which is the true freedom one finds in the Way of Jesus—a phrase I've adopted for this book that was in play during the early years of Christianity, and was used to define a small band of Jews and Gentiles who met in "gatherings" (the word "church," in Greek, is *ekklesia*, and it simply refers to an assembly) to think about the teachings of Jesus and to worship God in a manner he suggested. In the Tao, one finds a feeling of liberation from the need to conform to anything but the will of God, taking joy in the fact that "Christ plays in ten thousand places," as the poet Gerard Manley Hopkins so beautifully put it.

In my readings on Hinduism and Buddhism, I met the concept of the Self, or Atman—the eternal self, which is greater than the petty individual ego that Western thought celebrates with such destructive fervor. I found the difficult and complex notion of karma arresting, too: the idea that your deeds have consequences that play out over time in unseen ways. I began, for the first time, to think I should perhaps get on with the work of building good karma, as the consequences of "bad" karma can be severe! As a Christian, the notion of karma was, of course, already familiar if embodied in different language; it's a concept put forward (in his own terms) by Paul in his letter to the Galatians: "Whatsoever a man sows, that shall he also reap" (Galatians 6:7). I also liked the idea of dharma, with its sense that we all have a duty to forgive others and to act in socially responsible ways. Under the guidance of a fine young scholar from India, I read parts of the Upanishads—the primary teachings of Hindu philosophy—for the first time and found them inspiring. I still refer quite often to the Ten Principal Upanishads, in a translation by the poet W. B. Yeats in collaboration with a well-known Hindu teacher,

Shree Purohit Swami. These elegant sayings call us to a life of "auster-ity, self-control, and meditation." Some of these lines stay in my head decade after decade: "The Self is the Lord of all beings; as all spokes are knit together in the hub, all things, all gods, all men, all lives, all bodies, are knit together in that Self."[7]

Buddhism called to me with its concept of a Bodhisattva: the enlightened individual who recurs in time, coming with the gift of knowledge and ready with an example. I began to think of Jesus in a fresh way, as a unique version of this recurrence. It struck me as more than likely that such holy figures arrive in our lives as we need them, often without announcing their transforming presence. The idea that suffering (what the Buddha referred to as *dukkha*) is perhaps the de-fining characteristic of human life seemed evident as I looked around me. And I searched eagerly for ideas about how to cope, realizing I could draw on other religions for ways to add to my Christian think-ing. Wherever I turned, but especially in Buddhist writings, I found insights and ideas that I guessed (rightly) would absorb me for years to come as I teased out their implications.

Other parallels with Christianity caught my attention. I noted, for instance, the "ethic of reciprocity," which seems pervasive in all religions: the idea that you should treat others as if they were you. One encounters a version of this in Buddhism, as in "Hurt not others in ways that you yourself would find hurtful" (Udanavarga 5:18). This beautifully aligns with the teachings of Jesus, as in the Sermon on the Mount, in Matthew 7:12: "So in everything, do to others what you would have them do to you." This idea, as Jesus observes, "sums up the Law and the Prophets." It's the beginning and the end of ethical behavior.

There is something precious about the early years in a life, when ideas begin to coalesce for the first time, with a ringing of many bells. I realized in a primitive way, as yet inchoate and without sufficient detail to back up this assumption, that all religions pointed in similar directions, with varying emphases and inflections, as suggested by the

Rig Veda of Hinduism: "Truth is one, although wise men call it by different names." (I wrote this in an undergraduate notebook, perhaps taking dictation from a professor, but underlining it twice.) With this insight in place, I began to see that Christianity might still retain a usefulness, as the teachings of Jesus appeared to combine many of the teachings of other prophets.

I was interested, on the one hand, in spiritual growth—an inward thing, mystical in its goals: the effort to connect with God, to lose the small self and connect with a larger Self. I was also taken by the idea that spiritual growth only comes with what Buddhists call "right action": political and moral activism, the effort to look outward and, in small ways, try to help others and improve the world. This was all part of the work of finding the "I-Thou" experience in meeting others, as described by Martin Buber, and helping them if possible.

Quite early, in an introduction to psychology, I encountered Carl Jung, reading *Modern Man in Search of a Soul* (1933) and his autobiography, *Memories, Dreams, Reflections* (1964). I was stunned by these books. Jung's intelligent spirituality, with its emphasis on personal growth through an awareness of archetypal patterns and an appreciation for myth and symbol, led me to one of his American disciples, Joseph Campbell, who taught at Sarah Lawrence College for decades. With excitement I read *The Hero with a Thousand Faces* (1946), a book that proved immensely useful in my later work as a literary critic. Campbell studied the heroic journey in its many incarnations throughout world literature. I spent one hot summer as a student working on a road crew in Pennsylvania by day and reading *The Masks of God*, Campbell's four-volume study of world mythologies, by night. In a fit of enthusiasm, I wrote to Campbell in care of his publisher, and he wrote back with surprising speed and kindness. At his suggestion I visited him in Greenwich Village at his house on Waverly Place. Twice he came to Lafayette College to speak to student groups at my invitation, and we remained in touch for years. Campbell emphasized—in conversation, as in his voluminous writings—that each religion has a truth to tell, and that one should remain open to all forms of spirituality. At the end of the final volume of *The Masks of God*, Campbell suggests that our purpose in life is "to die to the world and to come to birth from within."[8]

In 1970, I spent a good deal of time reading and rereading Norman O. Brown, both his *Life Against Death: The Psychoanalytical Meaning of History* (1959) and *Love's Body* (1966), an eccentric if stimulating collection of quotations from a variety of literary and religious sources. Brown was a utopian mystic of sorts, a kind of latter-day Nietzsche (in style, at least), and preached resurrection: the resurrection of Jesus within us. It was all very New Age, incoherent and self-indulgent at times, but I found it wildly stimulating. In *Life Against Death*—his most coherent work—Brown put forward a rationale for an unrepressed society, digging into the writings of Freud, whose work was new to me. I felt strangely transformed by this reading, although my knowledge of Freud was inadequate to the task of evaluating Brown's interpretations. Nearly paraphrasing Freud's *Civilization and Its Discontents*, Brown writes: "What the great world needs, of course, is a little more Eros and less strife; but the intellectual world needs it just as much. A little more Eros would make conscious the unconscious harmony between 'dialectical' dreamers of all kinds—psychoanalysts, political idealists, mystics, poets, philosophers."[9] I wrote "Amen!" in the margins of my book.

I suspect that this account of my spiritual education in my late teens and very early twenties sounds weirdly systematic, as if I were some kind of super-nerd who spent all of his time reading. That's, alas, untrue. My reading was helter-skelter, and I relied on good teachers to push me in one direction or another. I read the books mentioned above partly in desperation. My early Christian experience had made me deeply conscious of my own mortality, worried about "salvation," and eager to figure out the right way to think, if not live. I suppose I had somehow established a base of sorts in religious studies, but it was a shaky one.

And whatever I had learned failed to help me when I found myself in graduate school in Scotland, at the University of St. Andrews on the East Neuk of Fife, where I had spent my junior year. Although I had adored my undergraduate year abroad, I was lonely there as a graduate student, finding myself in a state of despair during my first couple of years. I felt cut off from the United States, from my family, and—in truth—separate from God. No doubt it didn't help my mood that Scotland, in midwinter, is among the least appealing climates in the world: damp and drizzly, dark much of the time. I felt isolated and fragile, wondering if my literary studies (which kept me in Scotland for years on end) would lead anywhere. My prospects for getting an academic position seemed remote: the bottom had already fallen out of the job market. I didn't really know how, or if, I would ever make a living as a teacher or writer.

I still thought occasionally of becoming a minister, sitting in on lectures on biblical literature and theology. But my primary interest was in the School of English (I got a PhD in 1975), as I wanted mainly to continue writing my own poetry. This meant getting to know the poetry of the past as thoroughly as I could, though I regretted the haphazard nature of my education, which seemed endlessly provisional. As Robert Frost once said, we all proceed on insufficient knowledge. I certainly did, and still do!

Agitation plagued me, and I couldn't sleep. Soon I began to experience what I suspect were anxiety attacks combined with depression. I spent a lot of time walking by myself along the West Sands, which were windswept and icy, stepping through salty coils of yellow bladder wrack or pale mounds of seashells, fish bones, and driftwood. It became harder and harder to concentrate on my studies. Searching for help, I visited the university health center, where an elderly doctor recommended a course of electroshock therapy: this treatment was all the rage in the early seventies. "It sort of reshuffles the deck," the doctor said in a thick brogue, without a trace of irony. I fled his office in panic, not wishing to reshuffle my deck—at least not with electric jolts.

Looking for consolation and wisdom, I read (at the suggestion of a good friend) C. S. Lewis, and while I didn't admire his literal approach to Christianity, which felt overly familiar (given my Baptist upbringing), I could appreciate the merits of sticking closely to one particular tradition and actually practicing religion with intentionality. I took a little comfort in *Surprised by Joy*, a memoir that Lewis wrote in 1955 about his early life and his transition from atheism to theism, then to Christianity itself. I admired the concreteness of his style and his bracing spirit, which spill over in other books, such as *Mere Christianity* and *The Problem of Pain*. In the former, Lewis talks at length about a universal notion of ethical behavior, arguing "that human beings, all over the earth, have this curious idea that they ought to behave in a certain way, and cannot really get rid of it." Secondly, there is the fact that they do *not* behave in that way. "They know the Law of Nature; they break it. These two facts are the foundation of all clear thinking about ourselves and the universe we live in."[10]

At this time I returned to Tillich, always a lodestone, rereading *The Courage to Be* (1952), now with a feeling of desperation. Tillich rightly understands that anxiety lies at the heart of the modern dilemma, and this was certainly my problem. He suggested that anxiety might come from an awareness of one's finitude (ontological anxiety), a sense of the meaningless quality of life (spiritual anxiety), or simply a feeling of guilt (ethical anxiety). Each of these types of anxiety coursed through my system, but the combined effect was a distinct feeling of dread. I had several bouts of instability, although the experience went deeper than any easy psychological description. I felt alone in the world, and if there was a God, I considered myself distanced from him.

For a period, I toyed with the notion of atheism. I had a professor of Greek who found the very idea of God ridiculous; "far too medieval," he would say. It occurred to me that much of the world lived, happily or unhappily, without God. Religion had, in the postwar years in Britain, almost faded from view except among evangelicals, as far as I could tell. Between terms, I traveled when I could, including once to North Africa—Morocco, Algeria. I recall going into the holy hush of mosques, where I felt exhilarated and puzzled: the sheer devotion to an abstract idea, God or Allah, gave me pause. I wondered if God existed or if he was simply a human creation: a projection of some deep need to find comfort in a more benign universe.

It took energy simply to "be," as Tillich puts it, to accept that my life actually was something worth following to its end. Tillich explores the notion of courage from various angles, suggesting—at least that's how I read it—that one must edge oneself in the direction of self-acceptance, letting go long enough from the petty self to merge with God, whatever you think God might be. For him, God was the ground, the starting point of existence: you wake up and find yourself in the world, and the voice that begins to speak in your head signals the existence of an individual soul, and this soul in due course finds correspondence in the world, connections. You realize, after a while, that you are not alone. There is the community, and there you find God, with others.

My idea of God shifted, moving beyond the simplistic notions of my childhood, where God was just "father Almighty." As the harsh winds blew off the North Sea and rattled the windows of my frigid rented room at the top of the stone building in St. Andrews, I realized that I had no stability in this world and would never have it. I needed courage to continue, and I would have to work toward it with diligence.

I continued my studies, working on a thesis on Hopkins and the influence of Saint Ignatius Loyola on his poems, a subject that nicely combined my interests in literature and religion. There were papers of his I wanted to consult in Oxford, and I found a room there, in a building that was part of Christ Church College. I spent much of the fall of 1972 in that city of spires and college gardens (later I would return to Christ Church as a fellow). It happened that W. H. Auden—one of my favorite contemporary poets—was living there at the time, having returned from New York to live in Britain after decades of self-exile. A friend and mentor in Scotland, Alastair Reid, suggested I call on Auden, who was an old friend of his. I did with some trepidation, sending a note and reminding him that we had met briefly a few years before, at Lafayette College, when he came to visit the campus. He seemed happy enough when I called on him, and we met a couple of times in a café to discuss my poems. It was both intimidating and absorbing to talk to him, but he showed only generosity, and put me at ease.

We met one afternoon by chance in the High Street, and he sensed that I wasn't in good emotional shape, scanning me with his baleful eyes. He asked if "all was well," and I told him that I'd been in London the day before, where I'd felt overwhelmed by the crowds on Oxford Street—a roiled sea of people had swarmed around me. Dizziness nearly tipped me over, and I couldn't breathe. For relief, I had ducked into a passageway to shelter on the steps of a quiet building, removing myself briefly from the overwhelming mob. It took quite a while to gather my wits and get back on the train to Oxford—even Paddington Station had seemed more crowded than I could stand.

Auden listened patiently, then invited me to his ramshackle house, which sat unobtrusively in the gardens of Christ Church. I sank into a rickety sofa, surrounded by outdated sun-bleached newspapers, books, and unemptied ash trays, and within moments he brought me a large vodka martini without ice but cold. He was extremely patient and asked pointed questions as I further revealed the level of my distress. When I had finished whatever I had to say, he suggested gently that few people managed to find appropriate or satisfying meaning in the course of seven or eight decades, so it was no surprise that I found myself flailing. I must try, however. "I know very little, dear boy," he said. "In fact, I know only two things. There is no such thing as time. And rest in God."

I've thought about these two things quite a lot in subsequent years, attempting to come to terms with this wisdom, which floated in my direction at just the right moment. I knew I must get my head around time. This seems even more urgent now, as I'm near the end, not the beginning, of my life, and so time (or its short supply) has summoned my attention. I'm also just beginning to understand what it means to "rest in God," which I know means to "rest" in his presence, to take shelter there. In this sense, "rest" is a form of trust, and the word trust is exactly the same as faith, from the same Greek word (*pistis*).

Back in Scotland, I soon moved toward the Anglican Church, attending All Saints, where the rituals and the Book of Common Prayer lifted me up in ways that continue to sustain me. I also began to study New Testament Greek in order to read the scriptures with greater care. But it would be a misrepresentation to suggest that I began to follow the Way of Jesus, as I call it, without hesitations and indirections: these would continue, with arid stretches when I lost my way entirely. At times I felt downright hostility toward aspects of Christianity, out of touch with God as well as with myself, even distant from those I loved.

In my late twenties, when I was teaching at Dartmouth College in New Hampshire, I rarely went to church, preferring to walk in the woods beside the Connecticut River or read Emerson's essays or Thoreau's *Walden* when I required solace. Whitman's *Leaves of Grass* meant more to me than the Bible during those years, as did the poetry of Frost and Stevens.

After 1975, my permanent home became New Hampshire and Vermont, that area referred to by Frost as "north of Boston." I loved it, and still do. I think that's partly because of the natural world here, which is pervasive, invading your consciousness on a daily basis. For some decades I've lived in a house in the country, with nearby woods, and these have meant a good deal to me, as do the Green Mountains in the distance, which I see every morning from my bedroom window. Lake Champlain is close, too, and I spent a lot of time there, especially in the summer. I don't want to sound facile here, or silly; but I do find that certain natural settings are goads to the spirit, striking a deep correspondence. "Nature is our best teacher," the early theologian John Chrysostom (346–407) wrote. I believe that, and in the woods I'm emptied of myself, and find reflections of God in the setting itself, with its abruptly shifting weathers, and the moods that flash and fade with the dramatic seasons.

Since my early thirties, I've been going to an Episcopal church in Middlebury, Vermont. Stepping into that church I felt immediately at home, in part because it recalled country churches in Britain that I had found irresistible. My attendance was at first tentative: was this really the right thing for me? Shouldn't I just go for a walk in the woods on a Sunday morning? I quickly, however, found that the rhythms of churchgoing proved useful as a way of refocusing and reinforcing my own Christian beliefs, which remained somehow tentative and improvisational. I had no wish to return to the simple beliefs of my childhood, and it helped me simply to think of church as a place where I could "rest in God" with comfort. The hymns lifted me—the Anglican tradition is rich in music that I love. The language of the liturgy seemed brisk and beautiful. I liked the young man who was rector of this church: Addison Hall. He became a close friend and has remained one over the decades.

Belief is simply a fondness, a yearning: not a contractual arrangement with God. And churchgoing, which involves moving through the seasons of the liturgy, works a kind of magic in your unconscious, aids in the work of awakening to God's presence at the center of everything. The teachings of Jesus, for me, still seem challenging, new, terrifying, and profound. And so it's useful to hear snippets of the New Testament, to listen to sermons, to reflect on the language that falls into the category of scripture, although I think of poetry and many books of spirituality in much the same vein.

In recent years I've been drawn to the contemplative tradition, developing a practice of prayer and meditation. In this work, the Christian tradition of Centering Prayer (which I describe in a later chapter) has proved valuable, and I normally carry a rosary in my pocket, which means I can duck into a room and pray for a while when I feel the need. I can center myself by fingering these beads, saying the prayers to myself. In a later chapter, I will explore the use and practice of prayer and meditation.

Prayer itself came, gradually, to occupy a place in my life that has proved surprisingly helpful as an aid to contemplation, as a means of connecting to God, whom I regard as the center of being, a presence as much within me as without. As Hans Urs von Balthasar says in his stimulating book-length study, *Prayer*: "The person who prays not only stands before truth and contemplates it objectively; as John is fond of saying, he 'lives in the truth' itself."[11] I like this idea of standing before truth, living inside it almost constantly. At a dinner party in Cairo some years ago I sat next to a man in his eighties, a devout Muslim scholar. We began talking about prayer, and he reminded me that Muslims are called to prayer five times a day, saying that this practice brought him into the presence of Allah at such regular intervals that he never felt separated from his creator for long. I loved this idea, and determined to try—just try—to bring myself into the presence of God whenever I could, as often as I could.

But prayer is difficult. I'm reminded of a poem by Rumi, the Islamic mystic, who writes: "Don't do daily prayers like a bird pecking, moving its head / up and down. Prayer is an egg. / Hatch out the total helplessness inside."

With this advice in mind, I try not to pray like a bird pecking. I try to "hatch out" that helplessness inside, to strike at my vulnerabilities, to lose my ego-driven self. And I continue to read the scriptures—not only the Judeo-Christian scriptures but a wide range of poetry and religious writing in various traditions. In recent years I've gotten nearly as much from Rumi and Eliot, from Lao Tzu and Emily Dickinson, as I've gotten from the Bible. I turn quite often to a wide range of contemporary poets, and I'm grateful for any number of writers on religion, from Thomas Merton, Alan Watts, Thich Nhat Hanh, and Cynthia Bourgeault to Rowan Williams and Richard Rohr. There is a rich literature in the area that vaguely clusters under the heading "spirituality."

Most of the writers on spirituality whom I admire deal with pain and suffering in thoughtful ways, and this of course was compelling as I moved into my sixth decade. There is just so much to worry about, so much death to encounter and digest. I remember reading in *Everyman*, a late novel by Philip Roth: "Old age isn't just a battle; old age is a massacre." The sense of this massacre, combined with personal matters, has left me shaken at times. For a few years I was sleepless, or so it felt. I remember stumbling on a passage in James: "Consider it pure joy, my brothers and sisters, whenever you face trials of any kind, because you know that the testing of your faith produces perseverance. Let perseverance finish its work so that you may be mature and complete, not lacking anything" (James 1:2–4). This is a strong teaching, and it's a necessary one.

Of course the Christian idea of the transformation of pain into quick, abundant life has roots in the Hebrew scriptures. One thinks of passages in Isaiah about suffering (chapters 42 to 53 deal specifically with this), or the stories of Jonah and Job, just to name the obvious ones. Jesus represents a fulfillment of sorts, becoming the embodiment of suffering. Simply imagine his last words on the cross, which move from despair—"God, why have you forsaken me?"—to "Into your hands I commend my spirit." As Robert Frost wrote in "A Servant to Servants," "The best way out is always through." Jesus modeled this passage "through" suffering to enlightenment, to freedom. (As ever, I resist the word "salvation," preferring "enlightenment," for three reasons. First, it seems a better translation of the Greek word *soteria*. Second, it steps around the misconceptions about being "saved" that had been so prominent in my early days as a Baptist. And third, it chimes with my reading in Eastern religions, such as Buddhism, which continue to inspire and instruct me.)

Jesus didn't ask to suffer, of course; it was thrust upon him. On the other hand, he understood that in suffering himself he would have an opportunity to model a way through suffering. I know that I, and those closest to me, will experience disappointments, humiliations, painful illnesses, fears, nightmares, even tragedies. One doesn't have to look far into the past to see that history is a record of suffering. The world around us remains scary and depressing: at times I've felt upset and angry, even furious, wondering how God could allow such anguish to persist in the world of his creation. But I've come to see that the human path leads through suffering, that this is the field we must plow. It's the very substance of our lives, which we must transform, with God's help, into something better.

And God is, indeed, here to help: that much has become clear to me, and this help may arise in unexpected ways.

A few years ago, unexpectedly, an old friend who was a publisher invited me to write a short book in a series dealing with major figures in history. I chose to write about Jesus, seeing this as an opportunity to deepen my knowledge as well as my faith. So I set out on the journey to write *Jesus: The Human Face of God* (2013). The question was, where should I begin? And the obvious thing to do was to reread the four Gospels. To read them in a fell swoop is exhilarating: a kaleidoscopic experience, as the figure of Jesus shines through so many shards. This reading brought me closer than ever to the Jesus story, to the spirit of Jesus, and to the experience of God through him. I also read some of the parallel literature, such as the Gnostic gospels. I dug into the tradition associated with the search for the historical Jesus, and reentered the realm of myth. This was an occasion to return to Tillich, Bultmann, Otto, Buber, Barth, and many theologians I hadn't known about before, such as Jaroslav Pelikan and Hans Urs von Balthasar. For the first time, I engaged thoroughly with Charles Taylor, a modern philosopher of astonishing grace and wisdom. I read new work by Rowan Williams and others.

Writing this book put before me a chance to address old questions once again, perhaps in a more mature way: what or who was God? Was Jesus divine? How does one account for the miracles associated with Jesus, such as the Virgin Birth and turning water into wine and healing the sick and casting out demons? Was Jesus actually raised from the dead, and what does it mean to believe that? What is belief anyway? What about the Resurrection and its implications for the rest of us?

I couldn't answer all of these questions, and never will to my complete satisfaction, but I took a stab at it, with some arresting results— at least for me. I'm hoping, with *The Way of Jesus*, to continue this work of exploration and clarification, working for myself as well as for others. But I often don't know exactly what I think until I try to say it, so this writing—like all writing—is provisional, an attempt to frame what cannot be framed, will not sit still or come easily into focus.

As a child, I often sat among friends in Sunday school in West Scranton and sang a popular hymn titled "Do Lord." We were asking God to remember us "way beyond the blue." I hear that punchy tune in my head, and at night I will sometimes pray: *Do Lord, remember me*. This memory became a recent poem, "Do Lord Remember," that, to an extent, tracks my progress (and regress) in attempts over half a century to follow the Way of Jesus as best I can:

> Do Lord remember. I remember you.
> The petals of the pear tree you devised,
> soft blasts of light, blown white-asunder,
> heaps of blossoms on the grass around.
> The long hot summers sing your praises:
> all the lapping seaside shorelines,
> black rocks breaking through the surf like you
> break out so boldly in the slosh of waves.
> The oystercatchers always own your call.
> Each butterfly is yours, each moth and mouse.
> Each firefly, too, now popping in the dusk
> or, half-remembered, popping in my head.
> The fall is yours, that tumbling season,

with its mold and mulch, its yellow paths
through mind-ways opened and pursued.
You made the crystals on the parlor pane,
those dazzle-diagrams and fractal flares.
I do remember you in every month.
I'm not forgetful, like my foolish friend
who lost his memory midway and fell.
I'm not that old and toothless woman
I have watched go down your garden path.
It's quite a massacre, I must confess:
the dying generations, child by man,
the women disassembled one by one,
dear wives and daughters, mothers of us all.
I'm guessing you require so much destruction
just because you can, as doing does.
Don't get me wrong—my tone tips over
once or twice a day to snarky digging—
but I do intend no disrespect.
I believe in you, the ways you went,
your hands that lifted me along the hills,
that pointed out (in case I didn't notice)
many sudden turns I should have seen
but almost didn't. You have never failed me,
though I know I sometimes pissed you off.
I believe I'm coming back to you again
one day beside myself, perhaps in glory
or, if less dramatic, as a snail or slug,
a butterfly or bee, an aardvark or a dog.

You have kindly shown me how it's done,
and daily resurrections get me going.
I have learned to ride slow waves to shore.
There may be other tricks I've learned as well

in this good time we've been together.
Life is harder than at first I knew;
the course is long, blood-soaked, or worse.
I sometimes hesitate or stop to sigh.
Do Lord remember that I'm only human.
I have faults you've never seen before.
There's probably a touch of hubris there,
but let it ride. You're good at that, I hear.
Do Lord remember me as I do you.

TWO

THE CHRISTIAN MIND

- ## WHAT IS RELIGION AND WHY BOTHER?

The Christian hope does not lead us away from this life; it is rather
the uncovering of the truth in which God sees our life.
   —*Karl Barth*, Dogmatics in Outline

Religion has a bad name in many places, and for good reason. People
rightly feel suspicious when they hear wild-eyed preachers on televi-
sion who want only to promote their own brand while inviting their
naive followers to donate large sums to their "missions." They pretend
that if they give money, God will favor them with wealth and happiness. (This is often called, without irony, the "prosperity gospel.")
Needless to say, proponents of this sad strain of Christianity seem
woefully self-involved and blinded by the dream of affluence.

There is hardly any branch of Christianity that isn't tainted with
some scandal, from the abuse of children by priests to embezzlement
of church funds, so it's no wonder that questions arise. How can people behave like this in the name of God? And it's not just Christians
who contribute to the foul odor that clings to religion, as extremist
rhetoric (and behavior) will be found among Jews, Hindus, Buddhists,
and Muslims alike—the latter, a major part of the world population,

have suffered from the nihilistic violence that obsesses the worst elements among them, such as the Salafists, who adhere to a ferocious and narrowly fundamentalist version of Islam.

As my main concern is with the Way of Jesus, I'll focus on Christianity. A good deal of problematic history gets in the way. For starters, the Christian church grew corrupt during the Middle Ages, with political power centering in the Vatican, where all sorts of dark things occurred. The church began to sell what were in effect passes into heaven for one's relatives trapped in purgatory. You could buy the office of bishop or, if you were pontiff, make sure your relatives became wealthy. Beginning in the twelfth century, heretical views were suppressed within the church by torture: everyone has heard of the Inquisition and its countless abuses. During the later Middle Ages and the Renaissance, witch trials became a grisly feature of the church, and these extended to Protestantism, as in the infamous trials in Salem, Massachusetts, which resulted in numerous executions in the late seventeenth century.

With the Reformation, a stiff moralistic broom swept through Europe in the wake of Martin Luther's revolt against Roman abuses. The reforms of Puritan thinkers led, in due course, to the modern secular state, although any number of horrors defaced these reforms. The modern secular state was ushered into being by the Enlightenment, a period when the concerns and potential of the human imagination caught the attention of many thinkers, such as Hobbes, Locke, Voltaire, and Rousseau, and when the scientific method became sacrosanct. By the late eighteenth and early nineteenth centuries, supernaturalism gave way to naturalism, and intellectuals bowed before the altar of rationality bolstered by the experimental method. The idea was simple: one put forward a hypothesis, tested it in a systematic fashion, and drew conclusions that remained subject to further revisions as new information became available.

Like every reader of this book, I live in this modern secular state, and I appreciate the separation of church and state very much. For me, religion has to remain a deeply personal matter: the individual in search of God, within a faith community dedicated to the difficult work of finding God together and taking this faith into the world. I love that moment at the end of many services when the priest says, "Go into the world and do God's work." Christianity offers an antidote to the relatively one-dimensional "objective" or "scientific" approach to the world that is probably the mainstream of life in the twenty-first century, when (especially in the United States and Europe) Christianity has largely become the province of evangelicals. For me, Christianity offers a way of discovering a fresh sense of reality, a means of breaking out of the straitjacket of post-Enlightenment thought without negating the benefits of rational discourse and science.

Religion helps us to transcend our narrow, highly secular world, ushering us gradually toward a larger sense of love: the emotion at the core of the Way of Jesus, an emotion that begins with the individual and moves into community itself, first a faith community, then the larger world. The thin version of reality that most of us inhabit—I include myself here, though I work at widening my bandwidth of consciousness—is suffocating. The material world plays loudly to the senses, with its glittering surfaces and attractive noises. It's difficult for us to escape the material world, or to think how properly to *use* it, to move through it or around it, to occupy a space where one can hope to find that all-consuming love promised by the scriptures, the transcendent love that poets, philosophers, and prophets have foretold for millennia and that lies at the base of Christian thinking.

I've mentioned love, and I always tell myself that love is the most relevant term in Christianity, as Saint Paul suggested again and again, most famously in 1 Corinthians 13:13 with his call to "faith, hope, and love." Needless to say, love is a complicated term, often abused or misunderstood, bandied about in most religious writing and thinking, sung about in countless pop songs. It seems easy to dismiss the term as being meaningless, a mere multiplication of simple affection, a not-yet-kissing cousin of lust itself.

Love is usually divided, as in the New Testament, into love as brotherly love (*phileo*, in Greek) or heavenly love (*agape*). In common parlance, we think of erotic love (*eros*)—what Emerson in his essay "Love" describes as "the natural association of the sentiment of love with the heyday of the blood."

But I believe God's love, which will be found somewhere in each person, connects me to those around me. As Charles Taylor writes in *A Secular Age*—a book that remains a touchstone for me, one of those generative texts that continually surprises and draws me into its complex folds of thought: "In our religious lives we are responding to a transcendent reality. We all have some sense of this, which emerges in our identifying and recognizing some mode of what I have called fullness, and seeking to attain it."[1] Let me suggest that love is this fullness, and the search for love in the many forms it inhabits can prove both challenging and thrilling. For me, this is why one should bother with Christianity.

Needless to say, those wedded to secular realities also experience "love" or modes of fullness. They will suddenly be lifted by an attraction to another person, "turned on," drawn to fulfillment in erotic or emotional contact. Nature may delight them as well, as they see (for instance) a glimmer on the horizon when they look out over a lake at sundown. These moments of fullness or inspiration are numerous, if sporadic and fleeting, in most lives. But I would suggest that the response to these experiences is—in Taylor's terms—misrecognized. The religiously informed vision produces a larger frame, where these bits and pieces, these flashes of recognition, are seen for what they really are: re-cognition.

At its core, religion is about connecting to something already present, perhaps lost in the shuffle of our works and days. It's about reconnecting to ourselves, to others, an affiliation that is also a kind of affection. Broadly, religion involves a return to a "deeper"—that spatial metaphor seems useful if somewhat hackneyed—and more sustained reality, and this is where "love" occurs. Love is beyond us, or within us: it's that palpable kingdom of God that may make itself known only as a flicker at first, but which gestures in the direction of a flame, an all-embracing reality of the type that human beings cannot abide for long. And a religious practice—the subject of this book—involves allowing oneself to encounter this complex, harder, and brighter reality, the reality of love, again and again, however partially or, as Saint Paul says, "through a glass, darkly."

We Americans like to imagine ourselves as free agents, the inventors of our own independent realities. "I am the master of my fate, / I am the captain of my soul," they believe, perhaps even quoting the sentimental poem "Invictus," by William Ernest Henley. This is part of the ethos of American individualism, a bankrupt notion of individual action that has caused so much destruction in the world and has only added to our sense of despair. It's my experience that anxiety and alienation often follow when people try to control their fates and yet fail to consider themselves part of a larger whole, part of a living and breathing community.

Religion helps us to overcome alienation and the anxieties that come with it. But what is alienation? It has been endlessly dissected by modern thinkers, such as Marx and Freud, with a variety of cures put forward. For Marx, there is the material world that we create with our labor, and which must ultimately satisfy us, as we have nothing apart from it. We suffer from estrangement (*Entfremdung*) because (within the capitalist system, in particular) we don't see the end products of our labor; we spend our lives punching out holes or producing widgets that belong to some larger, invisible product.

Modern theories of alienation reach back before Marx and Freud to philosophers of the early nineteenth century, including Feuerbach, who suggested that God as a concept was itself alienating! For him, the concept of the Almighty opened an unproductive space between the human mind and its origin. "Humanity" itself, as a notion, was alienating when considered in religious terms, as it turned on a bifurcation: human/divine. As long as we're not "divine," we're lost, small, powerless. Another German philosopher, Max Stirner, extended and developed Feuerbach's idea in ways that soon caught the attention of Marx and, after him, Freud.

In Freud's influential vision, which continues to hold sway, we see a world of individuals who have been defined by repression, as the reality principle—adult life, rational society—attempts to thwart the pleasure principle, which keeps rearing its beautiful and seductive head. Civilization is by definition a mode of restraint, a system of programmatic (if unintentional) alienation. Society depends on the performance principle and trains its members to partake of pleasure in small doses or distributions, largely in the few hours when they aren't sleeping or working. The New Left philosopher Herbert Marcuse writes in *Eros and Civilization*: "A society governed by the performance principle must of necessity impose such distribution because the organism must be trained for its alienation at its very roots."[2]

In the late twentieth and twenty-first centuries, we seem to have normalized this alienation, and it overwhelms. It's there in our work lives, where we often live at a distance from those with their hands on the levers of power, who control our lives by corporate means of one kind or another (companies, organizations, governments). It's in our family lives, where the education of our children is parceled out to a range of authorities, and where even our sex lives are pushed into neat categories, overly described and safely categorized. The pleasure principle must, at all cost, be kept in abeyance, experienced in mediated forms, rationed if not rationalized. And the putative dangers of nonconformity are huge: chaos, anarchy, rebellion. These forms of disruption loom heavily and only add to our anxiety and alienation. Whatever else we do, we must not give in, accede to pure pleasure, become childish, undisciplined, ungoverned, and, therefore, unsocial.

Society might well be described as a formalized or externalized version of what Jung calls the collective unconscious. It's a rule-bound, naturally coercive entity or system of controls that often reveals itself only when we chafe against it. And society, as such, takes great pains to make sure we don't stray, putting checks on every manner of behavior, trying to control our intellectual, emotional, and sexual lives. Even our religious lives drop into neat boxes, in the little churches that live on every street in town, and where in measured ways the population gets to ritualize its need for "something far more deeply interfused." And secular rituals have been established, too: Sunday football games, for instance, where wild and dangerous drives channel into patterns, subjected to time itself: quarters and halves.

So what does one do about these alienating rituals and repressions? There is always the unhappy route of giving in, acceding to higher authorities or barely perceived patterns, pushing down something of oneself in the interest of the reality principle. Nobody really wants to live in a world where, like a crazed child, we race to fulfill every fluctuating and irrational wish, which is rarely more than appetite itself. Every parent understands the necessary submission to the reality principle that must occur in the process of maturation, during which the pleasure principle is contained, repressed, perhaps transformed into something "useful" and acceptable. This process is often sad, alienating, and confusing, and few of us know how to deal with the usual life changes, which are more like transitions than profound transformations.

I want to suggest that religion is worth bothering about because it invites us to understand submission as "letting go," a form of self-sacrifice that is liberating, even transformative, as it invites participation in the creative act, in that original moment when God said, "Let there be light." I'm describing a move toward freedom, not repression, that is governed by love, and that leads us into a greater love—for our neighbors and ourselves, for whatever we mean by God, which I regard as a transcendent power dwelling within us as well as without, something wholly other, beyond our rational selves, that surrounds us, forcing us into an alertness that allows for a deeper and keener apprehension of life.

Muslims seem to understand this release into God, having made it the center of their practice. The term Islam itself means "submission," which is submission to the will of Allah. This assimilation of the holy lies at the core of all religious visions, and it's frightening. I know I'm afraid, terrified that I will lose control of my life, the ways and means of my existence. When I pray the Lord's Prayer, saying "Thy will be done," I often sense my reluctance to give away anything or allow myself to lose myself, my petty concerns, my busy mind, my hopes and, yes, my fears, which I cling to in stupid ways. I become afraid of losing this much-vaunted "individuality," which our culture so prizes.

But creative submission to the will of God is what religious thinking demands, and it's what I hope to explore in the course of describing the Way of Jesus, a clearly defined path toward God. "The will of God is not a 'fate' to which we submit but a creative act in our life producing something absolutely new," said Thomas Merton, "something hitherto unforeseen by the laws and established patterns. Our cooperation (seeking first the Kingdom of God) consists not solely in conforming to laws but in opening our wills out to this creative act which must be retrieved in and by us."[3]

Ideally, religion summons that "which must be retrieved in and by us." It's about linking back to life at its source, in God, the creative consciousness from which everything opens into life and to which, also in life (through that mysterious door known as death), everything returns. I write as someone convinced that without a growing sense of faith, without practicing some form of religion, a person is (or can be) adrift, missing out on one of the primary experiences that life affords, including that of having a faith community. And community itself is at stake here, especially in this fractious time when religion seems (as with Islam and the West) to pose a point of fraction, and when it seems difficult even to see our neighbors and experience their humanity, let alone treat them as ourselves.

At least for me, Christianity offers something of value to anyone who submits to its disciplines and possibilities: an opening. God is the light at the end of this particular tunnel. Jesus doesn't represent the end or goal but a *pathway* to God, which is why he said, "I am the Way, the Truth, and the Life" in John 3:16, although in this translation one might misread this statement to suggest that his way is the only way. His way to the Father is a way to experience fully the spirit of God, a revelation of eternity that can be experienced only through time, in time, which is where we find ourselves as human beings, in constant motion, leaning forward, striving for transformation. And Jesus puts before us a way that makes transformation possible. We must, like him, enter time, moving through time to conquer time. This is the way that Jesus meant, suggesting: my way through time, with suffering, is the only way that any human being can take en route to enlightenment.

Most important, it's a pathway, and one far more flexible than conservative Christians are willing to acknowledge. Christianity demands what I would call "personalization." Just as any marriage has its own habits and tone, even its own language, so does any religious practice. The love that grows inside the believer—the word "believe" comes from a Middle English word that means "to hold dearly"—is distinct and personal, although gathered in a vocabulary that gestures in the direction of public understanding. It involves a return to God, to that luminous presence at the center of matter itself, which we call God. Usefully, the origin of the word "religion" (*religio* in Latin) tells an interesting story, deriving from the Latin word *ligare*, which means "to bind." I like the suggestion, which can be traced to the fourth century, that the word alludes to a process of "linking back," a return, a coming home. In this sense, to be religious is to reconnect to God, or a mystical source: to dig into the soil of our being.

In Hebrew legend, as in the Torah or (in Christian terminology) the Old Testament, Abraham is a founding father of the human race, and he linked himself to God through his willingness to sacrifice everything, even his beloved son Isaac, if indeed God demanded this unholy sacrifice. This tale suggests that religion asks something of us, as God does. He requires a kind of sacrifice, however difficult to define and embody. As Paul says, he asks from us a kind of self-erasure or "emptying out," in imitation of Christ: a rebuilding of the soul from scratch, based on the act of "turning back" on old ways, of opening our minds to the larger mind of God. (In the New Testament, a key Greek term is *metanoia*, which means "going beyond the present mind," although a mistranslation in the Vulgate, the Latin version by Saint Jerome in the fourth century, emphasized repentance, even penitence—a mistranslation that almost drove Martin Luther mad until it was explained to him by his beloved mentor, Johann von Staupitz, that the Greek word didn't really mean what he thought it meant.)

There is a wonderful aspect of "letting go" in *metanoia*. Change doesn't come without a sacrifice of what was there before, without a willingness to shift gears, face in fresh directions, imagining the way ahead without fear, allowing oneself to "unfold" in unexpected ways. It's an old idea, older than Christianity; one finds it often in Taoism, for instance. "When I let go of whatever I am, I can move toward what I might be," one reads in the *Tao Te Ching*. "When I let go of my possessions, I make it possible to receive what I need."

Jesus was a religious genius of sorts who, living on the Silk Road— a busy commercial route between East and West that passed, on one of its branches, through Galilee—had contact with travelers from everywhere. His teaching embraces many of the great ideas of world religions, and "letting go" is one of them, as in Luke 17:33, where Jesus says bluntly and memorably: "If you cling to your life, you will lose it. If you let your life go, you will keep it."

Metanoia need not be specifically a Christian notion. It involves self-sacrifice, giving up an aspect of your former self, turning in a fresh direction. Of course the Christian idea of self-sacrifice, as modeled by Jesus, involves relinquishing the old self, as Paul says in his letter to the Philippians (2:6–7), in which he suggests that Jesus "being made in the form of God" nevertheless willingly "emptied himself" (*kenosis*) and took on human form, as a servant, having been made in the likeness of human beings. This is the theological core of Christianity, its ultimate meaning: a release of the old, a welcoming of the new. When Paul talked about taking on "the mind of Christ" (1 Corinthians 2:16) in one of his most suggestive passages, he meant that we should imitate the behavior of Jesus, ourselves becoming like Christ as we face (as we all must) pain, suffering, and humiliation, only to rise to new life.

Sometimes this process of voiding the self is referred to as "taking up the Cross," a phrase which can sound dire, as if one had to suffer mightily in order to gain enlightenment. But in Matthew 11, Jesus himself says, "Take my yoke upon you and learn from my example, for my heart is gentle and humble, and you will find yourself at peace if you follow me. My yoke, I tell you, is easy. My burden is light."

This lightness of being should form part of the argument for Christianity, helping to explain why one should bother. It suggests an awareness of the limitless kingdom of God as well as a kind of leaning into the newness that has been promised. This doesn't mean that enlightenment won't require discipline and endurance. This is true of any spiritual growth, and it can certainly occur outside the formal boundaries of Christian practice.

My larger point, however, is that the Way of Jesus always moves toward transformation and renewal. "All faith is resurrection faith," writes Hans Urs von Balthasar. Whatever has been dead may return to life again, transmogrified in ways that can't be understood while living under a veil of faithlessness, which suggests a lack of trust in providence.

This idea is framed in another way by Karl Barth in *Dogmatics in Outline*, where he writes, "Resurrection means not the continuation of this life, but life's completion." He hears a "Yes" spoken which cannot be touched by the shadow of death. And so death is swallowed up in the victory of the soul, which recovers a kind of radical innocence in God, free from the torments and dismantling of time and flesh. "So the Christian hope," says Barth, "affects our whole life: this life of ours will be completed."[4]

The truth of such ideas about resurrection can seem difficult to access in our era of natural skepticism. Doubts about the "truth" of religion set in when it became obvious to biblical scholars in the late eighteenth century that the stories told in scriptures were a kind of myth rather than simple historical fact. The Darwinian revolution soon compounded the problem, changing the way human beings saw themselves in the world, not as complete and perfect creatures of God but as a slowly evolved (and continuously evolving) species. This concept unsettled those who adhered to a literal understanding of Genesis, with its vertical metaphysics, where God sat at the top and the ladder of creation dropped below to angels, then farther down to mere human beings, animals and plants, and even down farther into hell.

A skeptical view of religion spread among modern philosophers, from Descartes, Rousseau, and Voltaire, to Locke and Hume. The intelligent work of these thinkers made it difficult, even impossible, to accept a simplistic vision of how the world came into being. As it would, a reaction set in, and certain elements in Protestant churches reacted to skeptical thought by adopting a fundamentalist approach to faith that leaned heavily on revealed truth, resisting rational thought altogether, and leaning toward a view of scripture as the inerrant Word of God.

The well-meaning Christians who taught me as a child took the Bible as literal truth and rarely questioned the basic tenets of their faith. Notions about the evolution of the New Testament as a series of redacted or edited manuscripts that may or may not bear much resemblance to the originals didn't interest them. Revelation for them was a once-only affair, and this was God's Word. And yet revelation is ongoing and everywhere in evidence. One takes ideas wherever and whenever they appear, then tests them against one's own understanding. Again I must quote Saint Anselm (1033–1109), who wrote in a suggestive way about "faith on a quest to know," explaining: "For I do not seek to understand so that I may believe; but I believe so that I may understand."[5] In keeping with this formulation, I look around and see that revelation arises in unlikely places, in the radiant mist on the surface of the pond outside my house in the morning when I step outside to breathe the air; in a friend's moving way of coping with his cancer, as relayed over a cup of coffee; in the fragments of poetry that course through our life on a daily basis. I find myself drawn toward revelation in so much of the reading I do these days.

As ever, I find that reading is essential: I don't have enough ideas of my own. My thoughts frequently spin off the thoughts of others, and I feel lucky that so many other voices exist. Among the many gifted contemporary writers on Christianity, I take particular solace in the work of Charles Taylor. I first read him when he published *Sources of the Self* (1989), a wide-ranging book about the making of modern identity.[6] His critique of the epistemological tradition—that branch of philosophy concerned with how we know what we know, and with the nature of truth itself—is beautifully framed in *Philosophical Arguments* (1995) and, more recently, in *A Secular Age* (2007).[7] Taylor brings a thorough knowledge of the Western philosophical tradition to questions about religion, and why it should matter in this secular age. As Taylor notes, "Many of the spectacular battles between belief and unbelief in the last two centuries have turned on the challenge to Biblical religion from the universe idea," which he puts in contrast to the "cosmos idea."[8] In ancient times (as in Plato and Aristotle), the cosmos was conceived as a "totality" that was humanly meaningful, in contrast to the more secular and modern notion of the universe as an unwavering order of nature that barely impinges on human experience. The scientific revolution (dating from roughly the seventeenth century) discarded the cosmos idea altogether, giving us universal nature and its immutable laws.

The tug-of-war between atheists and fundamentalist Christians has become a spectacle in recent years, but I prefer to step quietly around this battle, which doesn't overly concern or interest me. To me, atheism and fundamentalism are two sides of the same coin. Both camps are literalistic thinkers, willing to accept a thin version of reality, dependent on the empirically based views of reality put forward by Locke and Hume. These were challenged by Kant, who in his *Critique of Pure Reason* (1781) noted the incoherence of this skeptical view of reality, which, as Taylor writes, "made the basis of all knowledge the reception of raw, atomic, uninterpreted data."[9]

All information delivered by the five senses is processed by the mind, and presented for interpretation and therefore subject to infinite versions, tones, cadences, and idiosyncratic conceptions. Further, as Nietzsche suggested many times, there is the medium of language itself, which imposes its own orders on the world, bringing its subjectivities to bear on our consciousness, our work of self-making. The fall of man is the fall into language itself, as Norman O. Brown once suggested.[10] The mind must interpret the world and speak it, bringing multiple perspectives into being. (Nietzsche did not dismiss the value of scientific truth, however; he regarded the kinds of objective truth that science discovers as a form of knowledge that must ultimately take its place among other kinds of knowledge. Scientific truths must simply be interpreted, like all data.)[11]

There is no need to live within the narrow layers of literal thinking. Rather, we can (if we choose to do so) cultivate a spiritual and intellectual life that embraces the physical and spiritual worlds in robust ways. In keeping with this, I will argue for a mythic view of Christianity in these pages, one that embraces the relevance of symbols for directing our mental powers, translating them into realities that can sustain us through life and, perhaps, provide a hope for something beyond the purely physical world—if not a literal heaven, at least a sustained view of eternity as a realm that may inhabit time in a "timeless" way, becoming aware of that juncture described by Eliot in "Burnt Norton" as the "point of intersection / of the timeless with time." There is a profound human need to understand this point of intersection, even to dwell there, allowing the mind to open to wider realities than those offered by everyday experiences.

My experience suggests that a desire for religion often involves a wish for a satisfying liturgy and religious practice, leading us toward a sense of fellowship and community. Ludwig Wittgenstein, perhaps the shrewdest and most inadvertently poetic of modern philosophers, never liked dogma, nor did he join a church. Yet he retained a lifelong interest in religion and understood the very human desire for ritual, once suggesting that liturgies were important gestures, like kissing a photograph of someone you love. I would go further, however, arguing that religion, especially in its Christian iterations, gathers and articulates inchoate feelings in useful ways, providing access to levels of reality that would otherwise be unavailable to us.

The pervasively secular world of modernity is numbing in its sameness and delusional self-involvement, its rampant and dehumanizing materialism, its moral confusions. Lives are lived hard and fast, with the stimulation of the senses being paramount. We amuse ourselves almost compulsively, in ways that exclude thought or regular meditation. Although I have no quarrel with the enjoyment of sensory life in all its splendid possibilities, this path ultimately leads nowhere. To a degree, any religious practice is about rearrangement, about moving from somewhere that was uncomfortable, incomplete, toward a life-embracing fullness. There is movement toward reexamination and redress, toward reparation.

Indeed, Hans-Georg Gadamer, a German philosopher, once described faith as "a process of correction"[12] in which our sense of self and reality undergoes continual revision as it moves toward understanding, and as it comes into contact with *logos*—the organizing principle at the core of experience. Gadamer argues, with passion, that each of us is "historically-effected," and that we can't break free of either our prejudices or the time in which we happen to live; but he doesn't see this as necessarily a bad thing, merely as something we must take into account. He criticizes Enlightenment thinkers who imagined they could break from prejudice and acquire neutrality, and he regarded the interpretation of experience as inevitably involved in community, in a community of interpretation.

Christianity is, above all, as I've suggested, about creating a "faith community," and I would interpret the word "faith" in its most basic sense of commitment: holding faith with a view, with a process. Rowan Williams, in *Where God Happens*, a book about the writings of the Desert Fathers, notes that these monks living in the sands of Egypt found that God "happens" in community. "This is where the desert monastics have an uncompromising message for us: relation with eternal truth and love simply doesn't happen without mending our relations with Tom, Dick and Harriet."[13] He quotes Anthony the Great, who said, "Our life and our death is with our neighbor. If we win our brother, we win God. If we cause our brother to stumble, we have sinned against Christ." As Williams suggests, we must see our brothers and sisters as well as what sits truly in front of us, with our vision unclouded by self-obsession and self-satisfaction.

The church as a faith community regards itself as the body of Christ, as God's hands in the world. These are common phrases, but they suggest an uncommon purpose. This was seen by Jesus as twofold: to love God and love our neighbors. "All the law and the words of the prophets hang on these two commandments," he said in Matthew 22:40. There are really no other commandments to compare with these, no rules to live by that override them, no dogma, no creeds above them. These twin commandments are actually one, as the love of God means finding God in our neighbors, and it involves losing ourselves within the community of faithful people.

Poets and philosophers, the Desert Fathers (and Mothers), in keeping with wisdom writers from a broad range of traditions, have tried to discover where God happens and how we can find a path toward "salvation" or enlightenment in community. The word used in the Greek New Testament is *soteria*, often translated as "salvation" and understood as "eternal life." In fact, this important word denotes an awareness of deliverance from fear; it suggests a condition of safety, a gathering of ourselves (independently and as a community of believers) into the larger mind of God, as well as in our relations with others.

The Christian mind (hardly a single mind but a gathering of minds within a broad theological spectrum) understands the Way of

Jesus as a path that opens possibilities for freedom in working toward "enlightenment" within a community of shared ideas and affections, always moving in the direction of social justice and action. We bother with Christianity because it brings us together, as a single imagined body, rubbing (often chafing) against others to create community itself. The Way of Jesus unfolds with excited, satisfying, grateful participation in the liturgies of a community and, beyond that, with the hard work of attempting to fix a badly broken world.

■ MYTH AND MIRACLE

> The need for mythic statements is satisfied when we frame a
> view of the world which adequately explains the meaning of
> our human existence in the cosmos, a view which springs from
> our psychic wholeness, from the cooperation between conscious
> and unconscious.
> —*Carl Jung*, Memories, Dreams, Reflections

In this largely secular world, where people commonly deride any suggestion of the supernatural, it's awkward to talk about a religion that appears to depend on supernatural events, such as raising someone from the dead or turning water into wine, among the many miracles associated with the life of Jesus. I admit to having struggled with this side of Christianity. As a young man, I found myself drawn to the fiercest skepticism, prizing rational thought. At the University of St. Andrews, in Scotland, I carefully read "Why I Am Not a Christian," an essay by Bertrand Russell from 1927 that he later collected into a book under the same title, with more than a dozen further essays attacking the religious frame of mind. Given my Baptist upbringing, I found this opposite course refreshing, even thrilling.

I still admire Russell: his clarity and self-possession, his vision of himself in the line of skeptical philosophers going back to Hume and

Locke, to Descartes, Spinoza, and Voltaire. Hume was the embodiment of the rational mind, and he wondered how we come to know anything (or if we really do). His persistent critique of religion, implicit in his major early work and explicit later, as in *The Natural History of Religion* (1757), set in place an antipathy toward religion that has been pervasive, especially among intellectuals, for three centuries or more.

There are cosmological and ontological arguments against theism presented in different forms and going back to the ancient Greeks and Romans. The classic statement of atheism is contained in the great book-length poem *De Rerum Natura*, by Lucretius, in which we are told that matter must be eternal, and that it therefore wasn't created by something or someone (such as God). Nothing comes from nothing: *Ex nihilo, nihil fit.* In the seventeenth century, several philosophers in England—Ralph Cudworth, Locke, Joseph Butler, and Samuel Clarke (among others)—delighted in picking up this argument, which had been given its modern framing by Thomas Hobbes, whose views cannot easily be described, as he seems to have shifted and rephrased his ideas in contradictory ways. Perhaps in *Leviathan* (3.12) he puts his views most succinctly, and this remains foundational in all antireligious discourse:

> Whatever we imagine is *finite.* Therefore there is no idea or conception of anything we call *infinite.* No man can have in his mind an image of infinite magnitude, nor conceive infinite swiftness, infinite time, or infinite force, or infinite power . . . And therefore the name of *God* is used, not to make us conceive him (for he is *incomprehensible,* and his greatness and power are inconceivable), but that we may honour him. Also because whatsoever . . . we conceive has been perceived first by sense, either all at once or by parts, a man can have no thought representing anything not subject to sense.

In other words, it's impossible for human beings, with their limited capacities, even to imagine an infinite God. We are primitive types with a compulsive need to venerate some powerful figure or figures. Hume and those writing in the skeptical tradition tend to stress what they regard as the irrationality of religion, often pointing to a universal ethical standard that does not depend on any divine source. Evidence is, to them, invariably material, and they rely heavily on the claims of empiricism.

Contemporary atheists continue in this vein. Unable to explain religious impulses and practices as more than blind faith, they rely on psychological or socio-anthropological ways to explain them. As it must, this path leads to wild assertions, such as Richard Dawkins's belief that there must be some sort of religious gene, a survival mechanism gone wrong but which comes nonetheless from the process of natural selection. Daniel Dennett and Christopher Hitchens tend to see in religion a kind of gullibility related to a basic human fear of being alone in an irrational world. They regard an interest in spirituality as suspicious behavior, even dangerous, as it has negative consequences, such as the endless wars that have been fought in the name of one religion or another.

In my view, efforts to say what is "true" or "false" with regard to theological propositions will inevitably run up against the limits of language itself as we search for an understanding of reality. Charles Taylor argues that what is "real" is what persists. If we can't replace talk about God with an alternate chain of words, if we can't replace God or prove him false, then God acquires a reality that is just as "real" as any other thing. Like it or not, this ostensibly secular age remains God-haunted; even by displacing God, one reinscribes him.

For Taylor, religion drives those who practice it toward ethical transformations and an openness with regard to transcendent realities. The latter is based not on fantasies or fears but on the intuition that what we see, the world of empirical evidence, is severely monodimensional, destined to enclose rather than open consciousness. Human nature, for him, can't be pinned down, though many try to do so. As human beings, we're inevitably stuck in social narratives, in stories about our story, in the social imaginaries we have inherited. Taylor talks about the "re-enchantment of the world" as part of the practice of religion, and he lays the groundwork for a remythologizing of experience, a recommitment to the myths that open rather than close boundaries and areas (ethical, social, intellectual, emotional) where humanity is active in becoming itself. "Religious longing, the longing and response to a more-than-immanent transformation perspective," says Taylor "remains a strong independent source of motivation in modernity."[14]

In the earliest stages of human history, thousands of years before Christ, people often imagined a supernatural realm where many gods and primeval spirits existed, some of them quite malevolent. Demons and devils, they roamed the world, seeking to control or influence those "below" them. By the nineteenth century, when the science of anthropology began to emerge, scholars (such as Edward Burnett Tylor) thought in terms of "animism," with the godhead scattered among countless objects and animals. It could well be argued that animism isn't really a religion at all but simply a way to explain the variety of phenomena that make up the world. But there were usually magical rites of some kind attached to animistic beliefs, with an implied mode of worship: a point noticed by the French sociologist Émile Durkheim, who in *The Elementary Forms of Religious Life* (1915) suggested that totemism, in which people identified with particular plants or animals, lay at the heart of the impulse toward religion, although others regarded this as merely an extension of Tylor's thinking on animism.

Polytheism may have evolved as a refinement or an elaboration of animism, with hierarchies of gods, as in Greek and Roman mythologies. And polytheistic societies were widespread in Africa and Asia, India, in the Middle East (Mesopotamia, Sumeria), and throughout the Pacific—one will still find them in so-called primitive societies, and aspects of polytheism survive in Christianity, of course, which often takes on a local coloration, with "lesser" gods existing (think of the ten thousand saints of the Roman Catholic Church). Monotheism as practiced in the Abrahamic religions was a later development, although one can see versions of it in, say, the Egyptian worship of Aten, the sun god, which dates to the fourteenth century BCE. (Even the early Jews seem to have worshipped other gods, such as Asherah, the wife of Yahweh, as noted by Rosemary Radford Ruether in her fascinating study of early goddess worship in the West.)[15]

In the nineteenth century, F. W. J. von Schelling argued in his influential *Philosophy of Mythology* (1842) that polytheism embodied an earlier stage in what he regarded as an intellectual progression toward a more sophisticated view wherein Jesus becomes the Second Adam, the fulfillment of all previous religious impulses. Like many modern thinkers, he regarded monotheism as a natural development toward a more sophisticated way of thinking. I prefer to see myth and miracle as pointing in another direction, one that makes it perfectly possible to accept other religious views, even to find them as complementary and mutually reinforcing, working on the assumption that most spiritual practices are grounded in the experience of individuals as well as social groups that have evolved a language that is adequate to their experience. We need many outlets for spirit: Mother Earth, the Virgin Mary, the saints, the Holy Trinity. All of these, for me, are subsumed in the larger concept of God.

I've always defined poetry as language adequate to one's experience, a way of talking about the world that makes sense. Myth is simply an extension of poetic thought, a systematic arrangement of symbols, an elevated pattern. One looks at the stars, for instance, and sees only chaos at first; but the human imagination begins to find patterns and legends. These well up within us, being part of the way we frame the world. We find meaning in these mythic tales, based on images. These myths are neither true nor false; in fact, epistemology plays little to no part in this kind of thinking, which really *is*

thinking. In post-Cartesian or post-Enlightenment thought, epistemology as the search for evidential and "verifiable" knowledge too
often trumps ontology, our theory of being, how we understand the
world in its origins and operations, even its ultimate disposition, or
teleology.

I define myth—in Greek, *mythos*—as a story that isn't dependent
on truth as factual or evidence-based reality. The Greek root-version
suggests that there are contours, implications, resonances that can
help us to shape our lives. A myth isn't just a "true" story; it's an especially true story, true in different ways from what we usually take as
a truth statement, such as "This is an apple." I'm interested in myths
that arrange our feelings or respond to them, amplifying our sense of
the world, taking us from vague intuitions (as in Wordsworth's "sense
of something far more deeply interfused") to a concrete and image-
based resting place. The Gospels are full of mythic moments, for instance, that have explanatory value beyond anything like a "true"
statement that is verifiable. Miraculous or paranormal stories seem
obvious examples of this, as the stories of miracles invite us to rethink
aspects of our lives and open us to psychological/spiritual realities
that we might otherwise never have known.

A myth is a rip or tear in the fabric of everyday reality, and huge
energies pour through these ruptures. And these energies often take
miraculous form. Indeed, life itself is the first miracle. Exactly how
we came to think, moving from inert matter into self-aware atoms
arranged in a certain fashion and capable of contemplating our state
of being, has never been dealt with by science or philosophy in ways
that, to me, are fully satisfying. David Chalmers, a cognitive scien-
tist, has memorably called this "the hard problem of consciousness."[16]
As Chalmers suggests, we as human beings remain troubled by our
awareness of ourselves as independent creatures with thoughts that
are divorced from the material world (the Cartesian dilemma), and
we perceive our alienation from this world of matter, even from our
own material being. We don't know how to proceed, and so myths

speak to us, offering explanations, suggestions, ways of marshaling our fullest imaginative resources.

Myth, as Thomas Mann has noted, "is the foundation of life, the timeless schema, the pious formula into which life flows when it reproduces its traits out of the unconscious."[17] But I doubt anyone has ever been transformed by "myth" in general. We need particular myths, ones that arise within local traditions, as in the Christian tradition, where the "story" of Jesus, the *mythos*, has transformative power for those who center in that narrative and body of associations. In their journey toward the gradually realizing kingdom of God, Christians focus to a degree on the miracles of Jesus, finding in them keys to an understanding of realities that might otherwise remain unavailable, the most singular of these being the Resurrection itself, the symbol of complete transformation. All Christian thinking is Resurrection Thinking, geared to rebirth. In fact, every miracle is a type or re-fracted emblem of the Resurrection.

Let's look at a few key miracles here and consider ways of thinking about them. The so-called first miracle of Jesus was turning the water at Cana into wine, as described in John:

> On the third day a wedding took place at Cana in Galilee. The mother of Jesus was there, and Jesus and his disciples were also invited to the wedding. When the wine was finished, Jesus' mother said to her son, "The wine is gone."
>
> "Woman, why do you tell this to me?" Jesus said. "My hour has yet to come."
>
> His mother called to the servants, "Do whatever Jesus tells you."
>
> Six stone water jars stood by, the sort used by the Jews for ritual washing, each holding from twenty to thirty gallons.
>
> Jesus said to the servants, "Fill those jars with water." They obeyed, filling them to the brim.

When this was done, Jesus told them, "Now siphon off some and present it to the master of the banquet."

They did what he asked, and the master of the banquet tasted the water that had been turned into wine. He didn't know where it had come from, though the servants who had brought the water knew. At this point, he took the bridegroom aside and said, "Everyone brings out the best wine first, then the cheaper wine after the guests have had too much to drink. But you have saved the best till now!" What Jesus did here in Cana of Galilee was the first of the signs through which he revealed his glory; and his disciples believed in him.

It's worth dwelling at length on this miracle, itself a kind of parable, or a story with analogical significance, one that is used to explain or suggest spiritual truths. Notice that we begin "on the third day," which suggests something beyond the normal counting of days, since in everyone's mind as they read this lies the coming three days of Easter, the Triduum, and Easter of course ends with the ultimate miracle, the Resurrection. It's about transformation of the most stunning kind, about the movement to a glorified body—from physical to metaphysical presence. It's about complete illumination, a final "seeing" of what in life is seen only "through a glass, darkly" (1 Corinthians 13:12). So we can expect something symbolic to occur from the opening words of the Cana story.

It's interesting that Mary, the mother of Jesus, points out that the wine is gone. She's saying: *You, my son, should understand that our people are in need of something very special. What is a wedding without wine?* Perhaps she sees the power of her son's transformative powers even before he does. In any case, he seems to speak to her in a brusque way, with some irritation. "My hour has yet to come," he insists. But she has subtly suggested that his time is now. He must act. And she has total control of the context, telling the servants (and us, the reader) to trust her son, to do whatever he says. Notice as well the presence of ritual jars, which were used for purification purposes by the Jews, and so would seem related to their religious life. They're made of stone, not clay. This elevates the six jars even further: these are huge jars, and we know the exact number, six. This focus on the details, number and material, enhances their role in the story. We must take them seriously. They represent the religious life of the community. And so the transformation that Jesus will oversee takes on special meaning.

They were filled "to the brim," which suggests fullness, complete devotion to the task at hand. There was nothing partial here. One gives oneself completely to the work, after which the miracle seems instantaneous, a natural manifestation. There is no wondering in the narrative, which proceeds with astonishing concision. The "master of the banquet" is an important person, almost like the priest at a ceremonial meal, and he is startled that the "best wine" has been saved until last, unlike in the usual circumstances, where you put out the good stuff and wait for the drinkers to get so drunk they won't know good from bad anyway. Saving the best for last is, indeed, a meaningful Christian message, one that befits a parable that is urging a reader to rethink his or her life and the consequences of faith.

For the most part, people move through life without a full sense of an ending or, worse, with a sense of foreboding. The ending could be, and often is, bitter. I don't think many of us expect the good wine to come last. But the transformation that occurs in this mythic story rests on a completion that is utterly satisfying. There is full realization here. The ritual vessels really deliver the goods. The "good wine" is the blood of Jesus, which is symbolic blood, and which reanimates those who consume it—an allusion, perhaps, to the act of communion, in which the individual participates in the societal meal, becoming part of "the body of Christ," part of the mystical body, and therefore becomes lost to the old, isolated self that has yet to be touched by transformation.

The story of the miracle at Cana radiates meaning, and I doubt that early readers cared whether or not the transformation of water into wine "really" happened. I feel quite happy to imagine the literal truth of all the miracles in the Gospels, but certainly don't worry about this level of understanding. Literal truth is the least important part of any miracle-mindedness. But one hears reports of miraculous healings, and one experiences—I do—the presence of God in one's prayers and meditations. I would not wish to reduce the world to irrevocable natural laws, as none of these can account for consciousness itself. I suspect we must allow the literal truth of miracles to fall into the category of faith, leaving it there, turning quickly to the more important, mythic levels, where these stories can actually change lives.

In many ways, the story of Jesus walking on the water, which appears in Mark, Matthew, and John in slightly different versions, offers a way into thinking about miracles, being itself a kind of metadiscourse on faith and the miraculous. Here is the *mythos* in Matthew 14:22–33:

> Jesus sent the crowd away after his talk, and he insisted that the disciples should get into the boat and sail ahead of him to the other side of the lake. Then he went up into the mountains to pray by himself. Later that same evening, as he was there alone, the boat began to buffet in the strong waves as the wind came up. The boat was far from shore now.
>
> Just before dawn broke, Jesus went out to them, walking across the water. When the disciples saw him striding on the lake, they were afraid. "It's a ghost," they said, and gasped with fear.
>
> But Jesus quickly said to reassure them: "Have courage! It's me. Don't be afraid."
>
> "Lord, if it's you," Peter said, "ask me to come to you on the water."

"So come," he said.

At once Peter stepped out of the boat, walking on the water as he approached Jesus. But when the wind picked up, he was terrified and, beginning to sink, called out, "Lord, save me!"

In moments Jesus reached out his hand and caught Peter. "You of little faith," he said, "why did you doubt me?"

And when they both clambered into the boat, the wind suddenly dropped. Then those who were in the boat praised Jesus, saying, "You are really the Son of God."

In the version that appears in Mark 6:45–52 and John 6:13–22 we don't get the part about Peter getting out of the boat; Matthew makes it more personal, so that readers will identify with Peter. In this telling we learn that the disciples' hearts had been "hardened" by the miracle of the loaves and fishes, when Jesus fed multitudes with a small quantity of loaves and fishes. This is the miracle or "sign" that precedes the walking-on-water incident, and it would seem they didn't like to see the natural order so harshly broken.

So this minimyth is about faith, about trusting that Jesus can and will be present as needed for each of his followers, and that the "normal" boundaries have in so many ways been broken by his commitment to love. Peter is always in the Gospels the most humanly vulnerable of the disciples, prone to excess of expression, eager to please, less than confident in his faith. "You of little faith, why did you doubt me?" is such a memorable line, and many readers of the Gospel will experience this question as an arrow in the heart. It's not easy to allow the mythic aura to bear us up, to let the water glisten under our feet as we proceed toward Jesus, into faith.

But the story is yet more suggestive than this. It's not only about having faith. Water itself is the medium of life. We're told in all three versions that the waves have been riled. The water represents mind and the medium of thought, where we swim as human beings. We live in the cage of what the Buddhists call "monkey mind." This is the untamed mind, where thoughts overwhelm us: fears, worries, anticipations, intimations of death, loss, damage. One can't even begin on the path to enlightenment without quieting this splashing, the unquiet surf. But Jesus represents clarity and calm. He walks over the waves. He isn't sinking into the depths, drowning in idle thoughts, terrible presentiments. The image of Jesus walking on the waves is one of mastery, self-control. It's a marvelous image that centers us as we read. The myth lifts us, allows us to "walk on water," to move into deep time itself.

The raising of Lazarus is another key myth worth examining in some detail. By the time this story appears, in John—the only Gospel that includes this stunning miracle, or "sign," as John prefers to call it—Jesus has come to the end of his ministry; he is approaching Jerusalem for his final three days and seems to know it. The village of Bethany lay outside Jerusalem, and Jesus was apparently known there, especially to the family of Mary and Martha, who have just lost their brother, Lazarus. Jesus hears from a friend that Lazarus has died, and some blame falls on his head, as he failed to make it to the deathbed of his friend in time to offer a blessing.

That this friend really mattered to Jesus is evident: the phrase "Jesus wept" reveals the intense emotion that surrounded the death of Lazarus for him, the only instance in the Gospels where he weeps. And the story unfolds in John 11:1–44 at truly remarkable length, one of the fullest narratives of a miracle seen anywhere in the Gospels. For the writer of John, this story clearly meant a good deal, and required the fullest of accounts.

Lazarus had been sick for a while, and after his death was buried in a vault with a heavy stone rolled over the opening. Martha wonders why Jesus failed to make it to Bethany in time to assist her brother, but Jesus ignores her questioning. He says, somewhat obliquely in this context: "I am the resurrection and the life. Whoever believes in me, though dead, shall live, and whoever lives and believes in me shall never die" (John 11:25). This astonishing response must have puzzled and annoyed those around him. Was he losing his mind? But his tantalizing remark suggests that some sort of transformation was under way. This is one of the seven symbolic "I am" statements that occur in John, such as "I am the bread of life" and 'I am the true vine."

The story unfolds with Jesus taking everyone to the cave. Lazarus had died four days before, so he was really and truly dead, his body already in the process of decomposition. Martha is worried about this, being a rational woman. Needless to say, word had spread that something was up, and people gathered to watch the spectacle, assuming that something odd or possibly miraculous might occur. They probably knew of Jesus as a healer, one who had already raised from the dead the widow's son at Nain and the daughter of Jairus.

With Jesus there, Lazarus simply walks free of death, stepping out of the cave, looking at the sun, smiling. Jesus liberated him from his burial clothes, freed him from death itself. Someone rushes to tell the Pharisees what Jesus has done, and this miracle convinces them that they must get rid of Jesus. Miracles seem always to make people feel very uncomfortable: the normal rules of the road have been changed. We expect to rot away when we die, not walk into the sunlight again.

It seems important that this mythic tale should occur just before the scenes in Jerusalem, with the Crucifixion and the Resurrection of Jesus about to unfold. As readers, we need some preparation for these points in the Passion narrative. One needs to pay attention to the rest of the Lazarus story as it continues. The image of his walking out of the cave occurs midway through the narration, so that doesn't end the story. Jesus and his followers go immediately to the house of Lazarus for a meal, a kind of celebration of the return of the beloved brother, who had been presumed dead. The Gospel writer makes a subtle point here: Lazarus sits at the table, eats solid food. He is not a ghost. And Mary anoints the feet of Jesus with precious oils, using her own hair to wipe his feet. In both of these gestures—eating the food, wiping the feet—the physical world is emphatically declared, elevated. John does not want us living in a dream world here—the literal matters. But the story is simultaneously bathed in mythic light: Jesus prays before he calls Lazarus forth. He needs God to effect this transformation.

The myth seems to speak to everyone who has been (metaphorically) lost, buried, and mummified. It calls to our need to say: enough of this. It also suggests that what we know about life and death is limited. I would put weight on this, admitting that I have no idea what it means to die. Nobody does, no matter what he or she proclaims. Faith is that mysterious force that allows us to bracket this uncertainty, to move forward, to step into the light and smile, to waken into fresh life. The Way of Jesus is always about transformation, about allowing for change, about celebrating change without limit. Love is an element added to the mix that gives hope: we lean confidently into life, into death, with some confidence that God will attend to our needs, will settle our anxieties, as we know that while alive we see only dimly the true outlines of reality. We are lodged deep in Plato's cave, and we want and need to exit.

I find myself drawn to the tale of Lazarus, rereading it anxiously, eagerly, hopefully. This is how mythic knowledge works: it seeps into us slowly. It undergirds our thinking. It makes it possible for transformations to occur.

Nietzsche once noted that "in sleep and dreams we pass through the whole of humanity."[18] Dreams, he suggested, carry us back to remote places in human culture, to our first thinking. And what is literature but dreams reified? It is symbolic thinking, and we understand myths because we've encountered them before, in sleep. We relate to mythic images in the Gospels on a gut level, and there is no need to worry excessively about whether or not it was literally possible to convert water into wine, to walk on water, or to bring a dead friend back to life. In story, all of this remains not only possible but endlessly available, and the symbolic thinking contained in such narratives enlarges our own sense of life, wakens us to what we already know:

that we can connect to sources of power that lie outside us, or within us. This is the work of prophecy—not to tell us what will happen but to say what already has. It's the work of literature, and it's the work of mythic representation. We read these stories, we dream them, and they become part of our thinking in ways that enhance us, that refresh us, that lift us toward new life.

■ PEOPLE OF THE BOOK

The holy scriptures are our letters from home.

—*Saint Augustine*

Almost every religion has a sacred text, even an array of writings that bear a special meaning; they may actually have a unique ontological status, being separate from other language, "inspired," even part of revelation itself: the Word of God. It's not for nothing that Jesus began his ministry in a family synagogue in Nazareth by stepping up to read the Hebrew scriptures. He read from Isaiah, one of the prophetic books: "The Spirit of the Lord is upon me, because he has anointed me to bring good news to the poor. He has sent me to proclaim release to the captives and recovery of sight to the blind, to let the oppressed go free, to proclaim the year of the Lord's favor" (Luke 4:18–19). And so begins the astonishing period of one or three years (depending on which Gospel you follow) of Jesus's walking among the poor in rural areas of Galilee and Judea, preaching his good news about the kingdom of God.

Those who follow the Way of Jesus should engage the voluminous scriptures contained in the sixty-six books of the Old and New Testaments. Some Christians read the texts more literally than others do and entertain different ideas about their status as the Word of God. I have long considered the Bible as a compendium of essential myths and suggestive poetry: a source of inspiration and guidance. I often read poetry with the same fervor and believe that God's revelation, in language, has not been "sealed" once and for all but remains, as we read in Hebrews 4:12, "living and active."

The Hebrew Scriptures

Many of the stories, sayings, and psalms in the Hebrew scriptures were once part of oral tradition: that treasure-house of memory and wisdom that was passed along by generations through word of mouth. They took written form only gradually, mostly after the eighth century BCE, when in both Greece and Israel the great oral traditions began to find alphabetic expression. In Greece, one finally got a text of Homer. In Palestine, the Hebrew scriptures found their way onto scrolls. As Timothy H. Lim says in his definitive study, *The Formation of the Jewish Canon*, "by the end of the first century CE there was a determined canon that was accepted by most Jews."[19]

For Israel, the effort to create written scriptures became especially intense after Jerusalem was invaded by the Babylonians, who destroyed Solomon's temple in 587 BCE. It had been the vital center of Jewish practice for centuries. Making matters worse, a significant portion of the population was taken into captivity in Babylon (what is now Iraq), where they pined for Jerusalem, as in Psalm 137:5: "If I forget thee, O Jerusalem!" A deep homesickness overwhelmed them, and the creation of holy scriptures helped to assuage this feeling. Editors or "redactors" began to write down what they knew, what they could remember, or what they could piece together from earlier fragments still in their possession. The process would take hundreds of years, with a good deal of reshuffling.

The Hebrew scriptures have three main parts: the Pentateuch (*penta* means "five" in Greek, while *teuchos* was a carrying case for scrolls), or Torah, includes Genesis, Exodus, Leviticus, Numbers, and Deuteronomy. These key books tell the story of God's relationship with his people, Israel, starting with the creation of the world in seven days. One encounters the stories of Adam and Eve and their exile from Eden, with subsequent tales such as that of the warring brothers, Cain and Abel. There are the stories of the Jews' captivity in Egypt and their forty years in the desert, the so-called Exodus, which centers on the search for the Promised Land of Canaan (and includes God's presentation of the Law in the form of the Ten Commandments to Moses on Mount Sinai). One reads about Noah and the great flood that overwhelmed the earth, or scenes of huge mythic import, such as the Tower of Babel or Jacob wrestling the angel or Abraham and the near sacrifice of Isaac. Narrative material connected to Moses and Abraham—the two major patriarchs—represents two central strains in these stories.

Exactly how the five books of Moses came into being has been the subject of discussion among scholars reaching back to the eighteenth century, but there is general agreement that at least four strands will be found: those relating to J (after Jehovah, whose God is also known as Yahweh, the anthropomorphic God who walks in the garden with Adam and Eve) and the E strain, after Elohim, another name for God, and one who is often gentler if more austere and mystical, as in the God who speaks to Moses from the burning bush). The J strain is associated with the southern kingdom of Judah, establishing the royal legacy that traces back to King David himself (often said to be the author of the Psalms). The E strain connects to the northern kingdom of Israel, with stories about the conquest of the lands outside Jerusalem (and no references to David). At least two other major strains were discerned, those associated with P, or the priestly class, and D, meaning Deuteronomist—a strain of writing that is associated with law-giving, as in chapters 12–26 of Deuteronomy itself. Competing ideas about the origins and composition of the Torah exist, though few doubt it emerged around the eighth century BCE and that afterward editors began the work of stitching together the various strands.

A number of historical chronicles of the Jewish people follow the Pentateuch, and these include Joshua, Judges, Samuel, and Kings, which tell the story of the conquest of Canaan and events leading up to the Babylonian invasion and the fall of Solomon's Temple. These "books" came together during the Babylonian exile itself, mostly during the sixth century BCE. This major narrative thrust in the Hebrew scriptures is often called the Deuteronomistic strain, in part because the language and theology of this storytelling mirrors that of Deuteronomy itself, a swathe of writing in the Torah that emphasizes the centrality of obedience to Mosaic law.

The prophetic books, called the Neveim, follow the Pentateuch, with the historical chronicles in between, and it includes the writings of the great prophets—Isaiah, Jeremiah, Ezekiel, and Daniel—as well as the twelve "minor" prophets, such as Amos, Joel, Jonah, and Nahum. Then one encounters the Ketuvim, or "miscellaneous writings," such as Job, Proverbs, Ruth, Lamentations, Ecclesiastes, the Song of Solomon, and the Psalms. Some fresh historical chronicles are found in the Ketuvim as well, including Daniel, Ezra-Nehemiah (originally one account of what happened after the return from exile in Babylon, although these form separate books in the Christian Bible), and Chronicles, which retells many of the old stories from the Pentateuch and brings the story of Israel up to the restoration of the temple in Jerusalem under Cyrus the Great, an important Persian king who conquered Babylon and allowed the Jews to return to their homeland.

The Psalms deserves a special place in this account, as it has been a massive presence in the Hebrew scriptures, as important for Christians as for Jews. These 150 lyric poems, or "praises" (from the Hebrew *Tehillim*), were sung by members of the tribe of Levi and used to welcome Jews to the steps of the Temple. They served various functions. Some were "royal" psalms, connected with ceremonies, such as coronations. Others were poems of lamentation, or poems of praise or thanksgiving, or poems meant to bolster the faithful, exhorting them to recall their profound connection to the God of Israel. Some are simply didactic, full of wisdom. As a whole they represent a complete anthology of human emotions, from despair and anger to joy and gratitude. A number are almost perfect in their expression, as in the twenty-third psalm, given lovely expression in the King James Version:

> The LORD is my shepherd; I shall not want.
> He maketh me to lie down in green pastures: he leadeth me
>   beside the still waters.
> He restoreth my soul: he leadeth me in the paths of righteousness
>   for his name's sake.
> Yea, though I walk through the valley of the shadow of death,
>   I will fear no evil: for thou art with me; thy rod and thy staff
>   they comfort me.
> Thou preparest a table before me in the presence of mine
>   enemies: thou anointest my head with oil; my cup
>   runneth over.
> Surely goodness and mercy shall follow me all the days of my
>   life: and I will dwell in the house of the LORD forever.

The psalms were mostly written in the sixth century BCE, and not by King David; indeed, most were composed long after David's reign, with some obviously written during the Babylonian exile. A few are possibly older, of course, and perhaps part of oral tradition. It's impossible to know exactly when a specific psalm was written, but they remain closely enough allied in form and content to suggest there was a group of authors who had formal affinities. Just reading through the poems in English one sees many repetitions, with a style that is associated with parallelism and refrains. I think of the psalms as, in essence, a miscellany of hymns that came into use during the Second Temple Period, after the restoration of the temple in the fourth century BCE in Jerusalem and before its final destruction by the Romans in 70 CE. Needless to say, the psalms remain central to Jewish and Christian worship, as they summon the faithful to remember God and his power, and many of them are hugely comforting and exhilarating as spiritual poetry of the highest level.

Transmission and Translation

Of course, literacy was rare in ancient times, which made it difficult for many to encounter the sacred scriptures in anything like a first-hand way. Making matters worse, scrolls were delicate, and before the printing press came into being, it was difficult to get copies. A language problem loomed as well, especially since Aramaic—a dialect of Hebrew—increasingly became the language of Palestine, which further distanced the Hebrew scriptures from their intended audience.

It was necessary for those who worshipped in synagogues to have access to *targumim*: Aramaic translations from the Hebrew. For the most part, worshippers experienced the Torah and other Hebrew scriptures in *pericopes*, which is a Greek word for "excerpt," its root word meaning "cutting around" a passage in the Bible. To this day, most worshippers know the Bible only in the fragments read in church or synagogue on the Sabbath. This is hardly the best way to get to know these scriptures, but it's the traditional method, and it has its uses, as gorgeous passages of poetry or relevant stories can be isolated and emphasized.

Palestine was conquered by Alexander the Great in 332 BCE, and with him came the Greek language (as well as Greek philosophical ideas). Greek spread throughout the region, including Egypt and Babylon, and soon it became necessary for Jews to have in hand a good Greek translation of the scriptures. This came with the Septuagint, meaning "seventy," after the seventy translators who gathered on an island off the Egyptian coast in the third century BCE to translate the Torah. In the course of the next century, the prophetic books were added, and finally the Ketuvim, or "writings," the third section of the Jewish Bible.

For Christians, one of the crucial developments in biblical translation was the fourth-century CE Latin version of the entire Bible by Saint Jerome. It's commonly referred to as the Vulgate, and was given official status by the Roman church in the sixteenth century, at the Council of Trent, even though modern scholars have taken issue with

some of Jerome's translations, which have some unfortunate theological implications. One key example of a translation problem, for me,
is the Greek word *metanoia*, which appears often in the New Testament and (as discussed earlier) literally means "going beyond" (*meta*)
"the mind" (*noia*). In Jerome, the term becomes *paenitentia*, which
implies doing penance, turning away from one's earlier wicked ways,
as in Saint Paul's conversion on the road to Damascus. The Greek
words *sozo* ("made healthy") and *soteria* ("enlightened" or "restored to
wholeness") in Jerome become Latin versions of "saved" and "salvation," thus shifting the theology to one of guilt and repentance leading to being "saved" from eternal damnation. Think how differently
Christian theology would have developed had translations of Gospel
writings about repentance been rephrased, so that "Repent and you
shall be saved!" had instead become "Open your mind to the larger
mind of God, and you will experience wholeness."

The New Testament

For Christians, the twenty-seven books of the New Testament offer
a guide to the Way of Jesus, with a compendium of ethical teachings
by Jesus and others as well as important information (in the four Gospels) about the life of Jesus and its larger meanings. Taken as a whole,
these books open God's plan for his people, but it was (not unlike the
Hebrew scriptures) a miscellany assembled over a stretch of years. In
this case, it was during the latter half of the first century that most of
these texts came into being, in part because they proved inspirational
to early gatherings of Christians in public worship and private devotions, which is why they were copied and recopied by hand enough
times so that they survived. (The earliest confirmed fragments of
New Testament writings reach back to the second century. The first
complete manuscripts date to the fourth century.)

It's worth remembering that the earliest writings in the New Testament are the letters of Paul, the first of which were composed only
a couple of decades after the death of Jesus (as Paul was himself an

exact contemporary of Jesus, although they never met in the flesh). One can hardly overestimate the role of Paul in the development of early Christianity. Indeed, more than half of the books in the New Testament are by or about Paul—a statement that needs one qualification: Paul wrote only seven of the thirteen letters attributed to him, those being Romans, First and Second Corinthians, Galatians, Philippians, First (not Second) Thessalonians, and Philemon. The other letters might be considered "school of Paul," even though they bear his name. They are often called Pseudo-Paul by scholars.

The authenticity of these letters wouldn't matter much if Pseudo-Paul didn't contradict a good deal of what Paul wrote. Paul was a revolutionary thinker, a true radical, and (although a deeply educated Jew) he preached freedom from the old rules of Judaism, suggesting in Galatians 3:28 that in Christ there was "neither Jew nor gentile, man nor woman, slave nor free man." What a marvelous teaching, a radical takedown of the old hierarchies that caused a rethinking of the entire system.

If you look at Paul's ministry you see that he lived and worked among women (such as Phoebe, Lydia, and Prisca), who served as deacons in the new movement and companions in the truest sense. He wrote to his friend Philemon to urge him to consider his slave Onesimus as "no longer a slave but more than a slave, as your dear brother" (Philemon 1:16). This sits in stark contrast to Pseudo-Paul, who writes "Slaves obey . . . fearing the Lord" (Colossians 3:22) or "Tell slaves to be submissive to their masters" (Titus 2:9). Women become lesser creatures than men in movement "gatherings" (churches) in the so-called pastoral letters to Timothy, and there are countless efforts to reposition the fiercely democratic teachings of Paul throughout the letters of Pseudo-Paul, probably composed by several authors—and perhaps written a long time after the original Pauline letters.

It always amazes me that Paul seems to have known almost nothing about the life of Jesus. He never refers to the birth narratives we associate with Christmas, to Jesus and his work among the poor, to his preaching in parables, and so forth. All that matters to Paul is that

Jesus was God's son who modeled faith in God for the rest of us, and that his death and resurrection opened a way to triumph over death. He was a radical mystic, teaching us to take on the "mind of Christ," to enter into God's kingdom now, as full participants in the body of Christ. He rejected the Jewish laws, suggesting that a brave new world had emerged with the coming of Jesus. Needless to say, his fiery preaching and travels throughout the Roman empire worked well, and the Way of Jesus prospered in the centuries after Paul's death, eventually becoming the official religion of the Roman empire—a development that would have startled Jesus himself, who never thought he was establishing a new and separate religion from Judaism.

The story of Jesus did concern, and fascinate, followers of the Way, and tales began to circulate. And so it was left to the Gospel writers to imagine that life, drawing on oral tradition and whatever texts may have existed, fashioning "gospels," which are hardly biographies in the modern sense but subjective narratives designed to bolster specific groups within the Jesus movement. The three "synoptic" (meaning "seeing together") Gospels are quite similar: Mark, Matthew, and Luke. Each draws on material that may be prior to any of them, a tradition called Q (from *Quelle*, a German word meaning "source"). Mark was first among them, written perhaps forty years after the death of Jesus; Matthew and Luke came later, but they obviously had Mark and Q open on the desk as they wrote, and didn't worry about copying from them as needed, often verbatim. Matthew and Luke had their own sources as well, and pitched their stories to different audiences, giving each of them a distinct feel. John, which may have been written many decades later, is utterly distinct, with many fresh stories and with the personality of Jesus seeming quite different from the man we have come to know in the synoptic gospels.

Mark is a blunt, stark Gospel. There is no Christmas story, no mention of Joseph or the virgin birth. Jesus is simply called a "son of Mary." And the ending is peculiar. In the earliest copies of Mark, the Gospel ends with Mary Magdalene and her friends arriving at the tomb of Jesus to find the stone rolled away. A young man—not an an-gel—tells them: "He has risen." The Gospel ends abruptly: "And they went out and fled from the tomb, for trembling and astonishment had seized them, and they said nothing" (Mark 16:8). This must have felt unresolved to many readers, and so ten extra verses were added at a later date; these include the great proclamation: "Go into all the world and proclaim the gospel to the whole creation. Whoever be-lieves and is baptized will be saved, but whoever does not believe will be condemned." That language about being baptized and "saved" fits uncomfortably with the language of Mark. The texture of the writ-ing, in Greek, seems clearly to suggest another author.

Now Matthew and Luke differ in their own ways. The former was written to an obviously Jewish audience, and it has a neatness that is notable, especially the fifth, sixth, and seventh chapters, in which the Sermon on the Mount occurs. The Gospel was perhaps meant as an early textbook for missionaries, for those who needed a thorough grounding in Christian ethics. Luke, by contrast, speaks to an audi-ence of gentiles, and the author is steeped in Hellenistic language and ideas; indeed, this Gospel frequently quotes the Septuagint, the Greek translation of the Hebrew scriptures. Luke's Jesus is both self-assured and clear-eyed, a compassionate teacher, almost a Jewish Socrates, full of wisdom and compassion. But he is a prophet, too, as when he first appears in public in Nazareth and causes a stir with such provocative assertions that he is almost murdered by the hometown crowd, who drive him to the edge of a cliff (Luke 4:29).

Importantly, Luke is also the author of the Acts of the Apostles, which is largely concerned with Paul's ministry and the question of how to be both a follower of Jesus and a good Roman citizen. In Acts, Luke suggests that some sort of reconciliation had occurred between those like James and Peter in Jerusalem and the provincial missionaries of the Way of Jesus, such as Paul. The former consid-ered themselves Jews first and foremost and stressed attention to ethi-cal behavior, to good works. (The Epistle of James traces back to the

Jerusalem church and reflects its concerns.) By contrast, Paul wanted to move beyond Mosaic law.

Now, John's Gospel is another thing altogether, a book that deserves close reading by anyone who would follow the Way. It was my father's favorite piece of scripture, and he carried with him a tiny copy of this Gospel from the moment of his conversion until his death. He understood instinctively that it was a stirring document, with lots of passionate language that can bring one closer to God. It famously begins with the hymn to *logos*, that mystical term that almost can't be defined. This is a true creation story, however; it mirrors the opening of Genesis, and it diverts us from the sweet Christmas of Luke or even the terrifying Christmas of Matthew. It brings us into a relationship with the Word in the sense of a deep spiritual communication between God and his creation, as embodied perfectly by Jesus.

And so Jesus himself speaks not as a man but as a mystical conduit to God. We get the "I am" statements: "I am the way, the truth, and the life" and "I am the light of the world." Indeed, John tells us that "the true light, which enlightens everyone, was coming into the world" (John 1:9). This light is private illumination, the bright spirit within us that is revealed day by day, as Emerson suggests in his essay "The Over-Soul," in which he declares: "Revelation is the disclosure of the soul." John's Gospel is the story of this discloser through the figure of Jesus, who is not in this version a man born in a manger but a soul on fire in the world, a bearer of the light. He comes to alert those around him to the fire they in fact already possess.

My own favorite saying in the entire Bible is from John 8:58, when Jesus angers and annoys his audience by saying, "Before Abraham was, I am." In saying this, he destroys clock time, chronology. He shows his eternal presence, which is implicit in the opening lines of the Gospel about the *logos*. God was before and after, and each of us—the children of God—has been present forever. Of course, Jesus also echoes the passage in Exodus 3:14 in which Moses asks God for his name, and God says, "I am that I am." In that passage, God asserts that he is essential being, outside of time. Jesus associates himself with this same God, the time-destroyer. And he offers a way to God through a deep recognition of this pathway to eternal life.

In John we see Jesus repeatedly discouraging those who wish to interpret him too literally. In John 2:16–21, for instance, we hear about Jews in the Temple who were unhappy with his overturning the tables, and they challenged him, asking where his authority came from. "Show us a sign of your authority," they demanded. He said to them: "If you destroy this temple, in three days I will build it up." They clearly have no idea what he is talking about and explain that it took forty-six years to build this structure. He lets them stew in their confusion, although John remarks that Jesus was referring to his body, not this literal place of stones. The cleansing of the Temple in John (unlike in the other three Gospels, where it's also relayed) is really about the purification of the heart. And this is just one of many instances where figures in the Gospels don't "get" Jesus because he speaks in symbolic language.

It's in John that we get most of the post-Resurrection stories, and in these—repeatedly—those who encounter the risen Christ don't recognize him. Absolutely central to this Gospel is the mystery of his rebirth, which is not literal. Indeed, the literal is destructive in John, a place for those with narrow minds and closed hearts. Jesus declares in John 11:25: "I am the resurrection and the life." He asks for "belief" in him, and this is the Greek word *pistis*, meaning "trust." You must put your trust in the symbolic language of Jesus, the mystical Christ, who can bring you into that inner kingdom, the kingdom of God that lies already within you. He can put you in touch with the fire.

Needless to say, I keep going back in my own head to that moment when, as a young student in Oxford, Auden took me aside in my anxiety and confusion and said, "I know only two things: there is no such thing as time; and trust in God." I think that is the message of John's unique and blazing Gospel. This is really the good news that Jesus brought to our ears.

The Whole Bible

It took a long time for followers of the Way to settle on these four Gospels and choose the letters of Paul and other texts that would fill out the New Testament. In the middle of the second century, a theologian named Marcion drew up the earliest list of books that we know about, and this included the Gospel of Luke (in a severely edited form), plus ten letters of Paul (or Pseudo-Paul). Marcion wholly rejected the Hebrew scriptures as belonging to the Old Covenant. Later lists included a book called the Shepherd of Hermas, which almost made it into the final canon instead of the Book of Revelation, which many theologians (including Martin Luther) wished had never survived the winnowing. Not until 367, with a list drawn up firmly by Athanasius, the twentieth Bishop of Alexandria, did one see the twenty-seven books now included.

A fair number of later gospels, the so-called Gnostic gospels, arose in the middle of the second century, and were full of esoteric knowledge, or *gnosis*. The early church suppressed these with astonishing thoroughness, and were it not for a miraculous and quite accidental discovery of these gospels in the sands of Egypt in 1945, at Nag Hammadi, we would have a limited awareness of this rich tradition, which includes the beautiful Gospel of Saint Thomas, a collection of sayings by Jesus that may well contain authentic material.

Sola Scriptura

The idea of Sola Scriptura, or "scripture alone," as the source of revelation and truth goes back to the Reformation and Martin Luther, who in 1517 nailed his famous Ninety-Five Theses to the wall of a church in Wittenberg. Luther was a devout Catholic monk, and yet he challenged the concept of "indulgences"—a system of pardons that could be purchased by the faithful for the remission of sins. His revolt against this and other corrupt practices led, of course, to the widespread rejection of Roman traditions across western Europe, prying open a schism that continues to this day between Protestant and Catholic versions of Christianity. Luther himself believed in the scriptures as the sole embodiment of truth, and he translated the Old and New Testaments directly from the original Hebrew and Greek into German, promoting the concept that ordinary Christians could themselves read and interpret the Bible. They could witness the revelation of God all by themselves, relying on the intelligence they were given to interpret these words.

Reformation Christianity was a highly individualistic form of religion, mainly about the salvation of the self, and it drew on what the Pauline scholar Douglas A. Campbell, in *The Deliverance of God: An Apocalyptic Rereading of Justification in Paul* (2009), regards as an intrusive paradigm, an alien and especially modern view of the world and its operations, one rooted in modern contractual law. As a consequence, this view of salvation (with its theory of justification by faith) has more in common with political ideas of the era than anything Paul, as a first-century Christian, would have understood or cared to elaborate.[20]

In the Baptist church of my childhood, the scriptures as a whole were highly valued, even overvalued. I was told that the Holy Bible was the Word of God, infallible, and the sole source of all true thinking. My fellow Baptists took the Bible literally, of course. As I began to study the scriptures seriously in my early twenties, I saw that the Bible was hardly a uniform document that lay beyond question and criticism. It had been written by many hands, many "redactors," who had assembled these texts over a period of centuries. What we get, in the end, is a collection of inspired writings that has proven indispensable in public worship and private devotions for millennia.

But are the writings in the Bible inspired? Of course. This hardly means they are "infallible," whatever that means. I would urge readers to approach them prayerfully and respectfully, yet with an open mind. Every story or statement in the scriptures demands context for interpretation, although "context" should never be seen as a way of denigrating the mythic truths they contain. Reading the scriptures can form the basis for a devotional practice that, when combined with prayer and meditation, will open the mind to encounters with the mysterious and inexplicable power of the Word, as embodied in the language of the scriptures, as whenever one stands face to face, in deep reverie, with God.

▪ SUFFERING, SIN, AND DEATH

The problem of crucifixion is the beginning of individuation; there is the secret meaning of the Christian symbolism, a path of blood and suffering.
—*Carl Jung, unpublished letter*

Nothing matters; everything matters.
—*Thomas R. Kelly, William Penn Lecture*

The Way of Jesus is a road, and it comes to an end: a final resting in God. Along the way are detours and pitfalls, times of suffering that may take many forms. The symbol of the road is not perfect, of course. I might prefer the image of a circle whose circumference is nowhere, whose center is always God. But there is no gainsaying the fact that, while in time, we move through time, and it often hurts. The hours tick away, and the calendar keeps turning. And, at last, "Time will say nothing but I told you so," as Auden once wrote.

In "The Dry Salvages," Eliot writes: "The river is within us, the sea is all around us." In this saying he accommodates two symbols for time: the river is clock time, flowing forward, not unlike the road,

THE CHRISTIAN MIND ▪ 79

attached to the calendar. It moves from noon till midnight, to noon again, from Sunday to Saturday, and so forth. Nothing seems to stop it. But the river flows into the sea, which represents infinite time. The sea absorbs clock time, becoming a symbol of eternal time, which has no boundaries, no direction.

In this chapter, I will consider three things that impede our journey to the sea, our final residency in the kingdom of God: suffering, sin, and death, which are interconnected.

Suffering

How could an omnipotent God, capable of doing anything, allow for immense human suffering? This is the so-called "problem of pain" that worries many Christians. As a teen I began to think it was impossible to justify the existence of a God who would torture and kill people, often in industrial-strength numbers, as in the Holocaust. I looked around and saw suffering everywhere. It arrived on my own doorstep when, on my final day of high school, in 1966, my uncle Gene was killed in a mining accident. It was a rogue mine, where he had gone to work because his large family—five young children—desperately needed the money. Needless to say, it was unsafe down there, and the roof fell in, crushing him. He was only in his midthirties. A decade later, I wrote about his funeral in "The Miner's Wake":

> The small ones squirmed in suits and dresses,
> wrapped their rosaries round the chair legs,
> tapped the walls with squeaky shoes.
>
> But their widowed mother, at thirty-four,
> had mastered every pose of mourning,
> plodding the sadness like an ox through mud.

Her mind ran well ahead of her heart,
making calculations of the years without him
that stretched before her like a humid summer.

The walnut coffin honeyed in sunlight;
calla lilies bloomed over silk and satin.
Nuns cried heaven into their hands

while I, a nephew with my lesser grief,
sat by a window, watching pigeons
settle onto slag like summer snow.

Like everybody else on the planet, I could move through the decades, remembering this or that horror. Suffering permeates our lives on every level, and our response to suffering defines us as human beings. We may indeed ask: How could this be happening? Is Christianity really a "tribulation system," as C. S. Lewis argues in *The Problem of Pain* (1940), a shrewd little book written as Britain faced the imminent threat of an invasion by Nazi Germany. Is God putting us through the wringer so that we can prove ourselves or show our mettle? Suffering no doubt shatters the illusion that we are self-sufficient, that we can take care of business ourselves. We can't, although pain and suffering may draw us toward God or push us away. For many, I suspect—those who absolutely refuse to believe in God and consider the very idea of the supernatural beyond the pale of consideration—suffering is simply a fact of life; it defines the universe in which we live and die, a world described by Tennyson as "red in tooth and claw."

The cross as a symbol for suffering is hugely important for Christians. More than half of each Gospel dwells on the Passion of Christ, which covers his last days. One moves through his final meal with his disciples, his agony in the Garden of Gethsemane (where Judas betrays him with a kiss), the trials before Jewish elders and then Pontius Pilate, his beating or "scourging," followed by his execution on the cross, surely one of the most barbarous forms of capital punishment. This is sometimes called "the scandal of the cross," for good reason. To nail a living man on a cross boggles the mind. And this "scandal" is a stumbling block to faith. Why not simply stress the excellent teachings of Jesus, as found in the Sermon on the Mount and scattered through the Gospels? Why not stress the love of God and loving our neighbors as ourselves? Wouldn't that be nicer?

"Nice" is not an especially Christian adjective, as the faith centers on suffering, on the cross, with Jesus modeling how to die. His pain becomes our pain, as we identify with him, taking on the mind of Christ in the process, absorbing his agony, reaching through it to God. In the most extreme cases of identification with the pain of Jesus, some rare Christians have received the stigmata, wounds that mysteriously appear in their hands. This is considered a gift by some. But I don't personally need wounds in my hands to feel his pain.

It doesn't take a genius to realize that every house will be hit by storms. Our minds and bodies will be assaulted, wrecked, ruined. Our families will suffer and disintegrate. Our friends will get sick and die. In this age of omnipresent media, we can't not be aware that millions are hungry, in pain, in parts of the world far away but near as well. Wars ravage the planet, as they have always done, and will do until the end of time. Global warming, as well as simple climate variations, create droughts and famine conditions that ruin the lives of the poorest of the poor. If you don't see the suffering, you're not looking. And Jesus, as the suffering servant of God, stands in for humanity symbolically, although not literally.

There is a popular but misleading theological strain called "substitutionary atonement," wherein Jesus is said to have died "in our place," as if God somehow required this grisly sacrifice to appease him. He needed blood to make him happy. This primitive idea, reminiscent of pagan religion, goes back to the extrapolated theory of "ransom sacrifice" put forward in the third century by Origen, and it has led to the notion of Jesus as "redeemer." That's a pervasive term in evangelical forms of Christianity, even though the concept is based on fragile scriptural evidence. I would reject the theory as a misreading of Mark 10:45 (also Matthew 20:28), in which we are told that Jesus came to "give his life as a ransom for many." That metaphor, deriving from the Greek *lutron* (which occurs only twice in the New Testament and refers to the practice of liberating slaves), has been woefully expanded, complicated, and abused to suggest that "belief" turns on an acceptance of this theory. Jesus did not "redeem" us in the sense of "buying back" a purity we had lost through the "original sin" of Adam and Eve.

That is much too literal, and it has no scriptural basis; in fact, it was a theory shaped by a handful of early Church Fathers such as Irenaeus, Origen, Tertullian, and Augustine, who reached back to Paul's letter to the Romans, twisting the meaning of two passages (Romans 5:12 and 5:19) to suggest a biological passing on of sinfulness. As a theological doctrine, Original Sin makes no sense, not if taken literally. (For that matter, nor does what is called Justification Theory make much sense: the Pauline idea—based on a misreading of Saint Paul—that Jesus somehow "paid for" our sins, and that we therefore must enter into a contractual arrangement with God that requires us to assent to a few statements in return for individual salvation.) A mythic reading of Genesis allows for wider interpretation, on the other hand; it helps to think of Adam and Eve as simply projections of each man and woman, and therefore susceptible to stepping across the line (transgression means just that) into behavior that estranges us from the source, from God and creation.

Buddhists seem to deal with suffering better than Christians, having put *dukkha*—a Pali word for "suffering"—at the center of their practice. They understand that it's necessary to experience pain, sadness, anger, anxiety, depression, and fear. According to this tradition, we as humans find ourselves caught in a cycle of suffering called *samsara*. We trudge through life in this Slough of Despond, as John Bunyan termed it in *The Pilgrim's Progress*, all because we can't quite grasp the true nature of the self. "All I teach is suffering and the end of suffering," the Buddha famously said. He taught that we experience this suffering because we grasp for permanence where none exists. We want to have it all, to lock in happiness in a way that it won't abandon us. We want our loved ones around us, and we cling to our good health, our good fortune. But none of these things is permanent. So letting go of the desire for constancy is the essential step toward enlightenment.

This is easier said than done, of course. "Letting go" takes a lifetime of practice. The point, however, is that we're destined to suffer. It's part of the human experience, perhaps its major part. And suffering can morph into any number of forms. It can be more or less subtle, more or less obvious. As a parent, there is suffering when our children suffer, often in ways that are quite difficult to understand, even recognize. We experience internal pain when a friend misleads, even deceives, us. There are countless ways in which one can experience emotional pain or anxiety or discomfort, and it's probably a rare day in our lives when we avoid all contact with any variety of suffering. All of these issue from our basic instabilities, physical and spiritual. I don't think anyone ever quite sits back and says: *Wow, this is perfect.* There is almost a jinx on such statements, as impermanence dogs us.

Yet even those rooted in the secular world understand that suffering is part of experience, and therapists are trained to help people deal with this. Buddhists often say that suffering is simply pain multiplied by resistance—a formula that many therapists embrace as well. The harder you resist the feelings of misery, the worse they become. Pain will always come; that's a given. And we must suffer from this pain. But we can make it far worse by fighting it or pretending it doesn't exist.

There is another aspect to our approach to suffering that should be considered: our inability to see any particular pain or anxiety-producing event within a larger context. I love the old Chinese story—many versions of this exist—where a farmer discovers that a fence in his pasture has broken and his horses, the primary source of

his wealth, have run away with some wild horses. His neighbor com-
miserates, noting that all is lost; the taciturn farmer replies, "We'll
see." Within days, the horses return, bringing with them an equal
number of wild horses. The farmer rebuilds the fence, watching with
amazement as these horses graze happily, contained; unexpectedly his
wealth has doubled. His neighbor is happy for him, remarking on his
fortune. The farmer replies, "We'll see." The farmer's beloved only
son now attempts to tame one of the wild horses. But he is thrown
to the ground, and one leg is so badly crushed that it has to be ampu-
tated. The neighbor arrives at the door again, saying what bad luck.
The farmer replies, as usual, "We'll see." Soon the country is at war,
and the emperor's army sweeps through the village and conscripts all
able-bodied young men. But the farmer's son, given his amputation,
is spared. The neighbor says, you're so fortunate! The farmer replies,
"We'll see."

This wise farmer knows that the larger story exists in a context
that isn't fully understood. It's a version of that beautiful Pauline
teaching from 1 Corinthians 13:12, in which the apostle suggests that
we now see "through a glass, darkly," and so it's impossible to know
what anything means in isolation. Human knowledge is fragile and
limited; real understanding will come only when we see God "face
to face."

As with the above quotation, I often turn to biblical passages to
understand the place of suffering in a spiritual context. In Job, the
ultimate biblical tale of human suffering, we see that afflicted man
draw closer to God in his tribulations: "My ears had heard of you; but
now my eyes have seen you" (Job 42:5). It seems that an intimacy with
God has developed that would not have been there before. Job can
now both hear and see into the deeper reality of God, where suffering
vanishes. Indeed, we are often lifted in our suffering: "I have tested
you in the furnace of affliction," we read in Isaiah 48:10. The notion
that God somehow "refines" us is an old metaphor, and it's a good one.
The idea is echoed in James 1:2–4: "Consider it a real joy, my brothers
and sisters, that whenever you face different kinds of trials, you will

know that the testing of your faith produces perseverance. And so let perseverance finish its work so you may be mature and whole, lacking in nothing."

In 2 Corinthians 1:3–5, we learn from Paul that suffering makes us more available to those who suffer with or beside us, and this is part of our joy and mission in life: to provide a ministry of presence, helping others through their pain. We are afflicted "so that we may be able to comfort those in affliction," and this is all possible because "we share abundantly in Christ's sufferings." This is another powerful teaching, and in fact the scriptures abound with echoes and refinements of the idea that weakness of any kind strengthens us, enables us to mature in Christ, to come closer to him and, through him and the example of his suffering, closer to God.

Just as Jesus leaned into his suffering, so should we. The only way out is through, and this involves accepting what lies before us, staying with it, understanding its origins, and being aware that trust in God means accepting that our fate lies in his hands. "Thy will be done" is always the essential prayer in difficult times, a way into and through the crisis. As Quaker writer Thomas R. Kelly writes, part of the fruit of holy obedience is entrance into suffering. "I would not magnify joy and rapture, although they are unspeakably great in the committed life," he says. "For joy and rapture need no advocates. But we shrink from suffering and can easily call all suffering an evil thing." He invites us to ponder a paradox in religious experience: "Nothing matters; everything matters." As he says, this paradox offers the key of entrance into suffering. "He who knows only one-half of the paradox can never enter that door of mystery and survive."

Sin

It's worth considering the idea of sin in the context of suffering. Does God really punish us because we "misbehave" in some way? Many people, even those without any faith, believe that when they suffer it must be their fault. Even worse, they assume that others suffer because it's *their* fault. The poor are poor, for instance, because they failed to work hard enough or to foresee economic problems. Those who fall ill or have accidents do so because God wishes to punish them. Versions of this benighted notion ripple through American society and afflict our politics, a residue of a Puritan heritage.

Many preachers in Colonial America agreed with Benjamin Wadsworth, who argued that people "should most seriously consider and acknowledge, that it is the Great God who brings Sickness upon them." He went even further: "He prevents them, sends them, removes them just as he will. All our bodily illnesses and ailments whatsoever, are ordered forth by God."[21] Sickness, poverty, misery of any kind: these were the consequences of our iniquities, our laziness, our lack of due diligence before God, who holds bad things in reserve to remind us of our dependence on him.

This may be traced to the Calvinist idea that God has chosen certain people (the elect) for wealth and good health, while he has condemned others to poverty and illness. This idea roots in the subsoil of the American unconscious, and it pervades our thinking about wealth and poverty, about health and sickness, and it affects our everyday politics in negative ways. The ideas of social Darwinism, especially the concept of "the survival of the fittest" (as put forward by Herbert Spencer), have converged with our Puritan heritage, emerging in distinctly cruel formulations, as with Ayn Rand, the Russian American novelist, with her infamous celebration of self-centered behavior: "Nobody is mine." This is hardly what Jesus taught or modeled in his earthly life, where he dwelled among the poor, saying that the "last shall be first" (Matthew 20:16). Everybody was his.

So what about sin and punishment? What about hell itself, the ultimate place where the sinner must (in some theological strains of Christianity) suffer eternal torment? I like to think of sin as "error." It's so easy to be tempted by one thing or another: sin involves stepping off the "right" or "straight" path—the word "right" derives from an Anglo-Saxon word that means the straight route from one point on the map to another. The "wrong" way is the "crooked" or "round-about" path. Evil is a misstep, a move in the wrong direction. This perhaps seems anodyne, a way of talking that attempts to downplay evil, which is very real.

There are damaged or afflicted minds, people who can see only darkness and therefore create, or try to create, darkness all around them, bringing the world down on their heads and the heads of others. I would put monstrous dictators like Hitler and Stalin, Mao, Idi Amin and Pol Pot, as well as serial killers and sadistic rapists into this category. These are extreme examples, but they can't be denied. For the most part, however, our sinful behavior isn't so horrendously evil. We simply fail to treat others as we would treat ourselves. And this is the "sin," or error, that leads to "hell," which is merely separation from God, which begins with separation from our neighbors.

The Gospels load evil into the totalizing figure of Satan. In the Gospels, Jesus struggles with the Evil One in the desert. There are (extremely occasional) references to the Devil throughout the Bible, and sometimes these are obviously metaphorical, sometimes not. For the most part, Satan—the term derives from the Hebrew *ha-satan*, which means "the Adversary"—is not embodied as an actual creature; he is the "stumbling block," as in Matthew 16:23, where Jesus says to Peter: "Get behind me, Satan!" That's just a bad translation of "stumbling block"—my preferred translation of the Greek word for the Adversary. Whether or not one personifies or mythologizes the adversarial principle as a creature depends on the level of literalness one wishes to achieve. I would look to the larger *mythos* here.

We all stray from the path we know is the right one now and then, and sometimes we blow wildly off course, doing real damage to others and, ultimately, to ourselves. Again, the point of the *mythos*, the story of Jesus, is to provide direction, as Thomas à Kempis suggests at the opening of *The Imitation of Christ*, a Christian handbook from the early fifteenth century that, after the Bible itself, has been the most widely read book in Christendom: "'He who follows Me, walks not in darkness,' says the Lord. By these words of Christ we are advised to imitate His life and habits, if we wish to be truly enlightened and free from all blindness of heart." [22]

It's not for nothing that Jesus taught us to pray: "Forgive us our trespasses, as we forgive those who trespass against us." This is the beginning and, perhaps, the end of all wisdom. Forgiving: the embodiment of love, its perfect expression, occurs when Jesus on the cross said, "Father, forgive them, for they know not what they do." And it's the way back to mental health, to wholeness, to reconciliation with our creator and, through him, with creation itself.

Death

The fear of death disturbs, unsettles, and torments us. And yet the fact of our mortality seems part of the myth of Adam and Eve. There they were, in the first two chapters of Genesis, enjoying eternal life in their present and perfect world. Only their fatal error, stepping off the path, crossing a line by disobeying God, created their mortality. God sent them out, east of Eden, into the fallen world.

I often recite in my head the final glorious but sad lines from Book XII of Milton's *Paradise Lost*, where we see Adam and Eve setting forth into exile:

> They looking back, all the Eastern side beheld
> Of Paradise, so late their happy seat,
> Waved over by that flaming Brand, the Gate
> With dreadful Faces thronged and fiery armies:
> Some natural tears they dropped, but wiped them soon.
> The World was all before them, where to choose
> Their place of rest, and Providence their guide:
> They hand in hand with wandering steps and slow,
> Through Eden took their solitary way.

Their fate is to experience suffering, sin, and death. They become mortal. And this myth can't help but make us ask the big question: why? The Christian answer runs like this: God gave human beings free will, a freedom to choose their fate; they may behave well or badly. It's a kind of blistering freedom, where many fall by the wayside. Evil—certainly in Milton's view—affords an opportunity for recovery. When Adam gets to stand apart and see the whole of human history, he regards the fall of man as a "happy fault," allowing God to show his mercy, to display compassion through the gift of his son. This does, however, feel simplistic, and it probably does little to help us when we think about death: our own death, the death of our parents and loved ones. The fear of death isn't easily driven away by rationalizations about free will being something special. Maybe we'd prefer the security of eternal life in the Garden of Eden to the dizzy-making freedom we experience in this brief life?

Pascal, one of the finest Christian philosophers, wrote: "All I know is that I must soon die; but what I know least is this very death which I cannot escape." This is our paradoxical state: we know we are dust, and to dust we return. Nobody is here for long, and everything points to this end. Most days, we avert our eyes from mortality. We pretend nothing is amiss. But everything is amiss, if you think of death as a tragedy. Only when a close friend or relative dies do we, for a short time, contemplate the end of life, which for the most part is treated as a scandal itself, something unmentionable, although children get it. Every one of my three sons at a certain age inquired about death with deep concern. And I had no easy answers, no comforting responses. But this question is not something one should dismiss or gloss over.

Fundamentalist Christians like to imagine heaven as a physical place where the streets are paved with gold, where we gather in eternal life singing to God our hymns of praise. I remember hearing this sketch of heaven in church with some alarm. I didn't want to sing in that heavenly choir, and it struck me as almost as bad as the alternative literalist view: burning in hell. Happily I could dismiss these notions of heaven and hell rather easily. The idea of vertical reality, with heaven above us and hell below, seemed quite wrong. And the mystery of death struck me as something I could hardly hope to penetrate. I don't know if I'm any further along today than I was then, at fourteen or fifteen, at least when it comes to understanding mortality and the afterlife.

I stumbled upon a short essay by Emerson years ago, and this set off a train of thought that continues to prove useful in my later decades. In "Immortality" (1876), he notes that the future state we might imagine "is an illusion for the ever-present state. It is not a length of life but a depth of life" that matters. The spiritual world simply "takes place," and this provides our immortality. "Jesus explained nothing," Emerson says, "but the influence of him took people out of time, and they felt eternal. A great integrity makes us immortal; an admiration, a deep love, a strong will arms us above fear. It makes a day memorable. We say we lived years in that hour. It is strange that Jesus is esteemed by mankind the bringer of the doctrine of immortality. He is never once weak or sentimental; he is very abstemious of explanation."

Not length of life but depth. The key lies there. We must reconceive how time plays out and move beyond time, into no-time, the eternity of the larger Self, connecting to the God within us; there we may find immortality. The kingdom of God is within us, as Jesus said, and we ultimately rest there. And the good news is that we can begin now.

While Jesus said very little about immortality, Paul commented vividly on the Resurrection in 1 Corinthians 15:35–44:

> Somebody will ask, "How are the dead raised? With what kind of body will they have after death?" What a foolish question! What you sow doesn't come to life unless it dies. When you sow, you do not plant the body that will be, but just a seed, perhaps of wheat or of something else. But

God gives it a body as he has planned it, and to each kind
of seed he gives its own body. Not all flesh is the same:
People have one kind of flesh, animals have another,
birds another and fish another. There are also heavenly
bodies and there are earthly bodies; but the splendor of
the heavenly bodies is one kind, and the splendor of the
earthly bodies is another. The sun has one kind of splendor, the moon another and the stars another; and star
differs from star in splendor.

So it will be with the resurrection of the dead. The
body that is sown is perishable, it is raised imperishable;
it is sown in shame, it is raised in glory; it is sown in
weakness, it is raised in power; it is sown a natural body,
it is raised a spiritual body.

In an age-old tradition, Paul associates the death of a person with
the death of a plant, linking human life with the natural world, the
cycle of seasons. We become seeds again, planted in the earth. Like
a plant, with its roots underground, we stir in spring, and we are
"raised" by the sun, fed by the fresh waters to gurgle in the subsoil.
And the "spiritual body" we assume in the afterlife can't easily be
compared to the body we leave behind. It's new, a "glorified body,"
something we can't begin to understand.

When I worry about my own death or the death of my wife, my
children, my family, or friends, I ask myself: do I really want this to
last? Of course I love my wife and family intensely, and I passionately
hope to have their good company in the afterlife.

But where is the afterlife?

The fact remains that we can't know what death will bring or fully
appreciate the meaning of human suffering. These are great mysteries. As with the Chinese farmer in the story above, we must wait and
see. But we can do this hopefully, perhaps joyfully, as we learn to live
(and lean) deeply into the present, growing closer to God through

the practice of our faith, moving closer to the Way of Jesus, finding its grooves and reveling in them. Our practice brings us closer to immortality itself—a state of "here, now, always."

▪ THE SERMON ON THE MOUNT

I saw that the Sermon on the Mount was the whole of the Christianity for those who wanted to live a Christian life.
—*Gandhi, "The Jesus I Love"*

The core teachings of Jesus were neatly arranged in the fifth, sixth, and seventh chapters of Matthew. This extended passage is called the Sermon on the Mount, and it puts forward a radical message that has reverberated down centuries. Few sermons in the history of the world contain so much compressed wisdom or have been so influential. Without these teachings, one would have to intuit the ideas of Jesus from occasional sayings and parables scattered throughout the four Gospels; but this is a brilliant sequence of related ethical teachings, assembled a few decades after the death of Jesus by one of his evangelists.

Jesus drew his disciples to a hilltop in Galilee—with shades of Moses, another specialist in mountain wisdom. With a large audience at his feet, he presents the Beatitudes, these succinct and moving "sayings." This is obviously a literary construct, as nobody talks in such a stilted way, and one needn't worry about the fact that it's a construct: the Gospels are all constructs, texts woven from a combination of oral history and textual material. Overall, the Sermon on the Mount reminds us that Jesus was first and foremost a teacher. When Mary Magdalene visited him in the tomb on Easter morning—the first person to encounter him after the Resurrection—she didn't recognize him until he spoke her name, "Mary." At that point, she replied in Aramaic: "*Rabboni!*" He was her teacher, which is what that term means.

The Beatitudes consist of nine definitive statements. Each has a simple formula: Blessed are X, for they shall be rewarded in kind. Here are the sayings, in the beautiful King James Version:

> Blessed are the poor in spirit: for theirs is the kingdom
> of heaven.
> Blessed are they that mourn: for they shall be comforted.
> Blessed are the meek: for they shall inherit the earth.
> Blessed are they which do hunger and thirst after righteousness:
> for they shall be filled.
> Blessed are the merciful: for they shall obtain mercy.
> Blessed are the pure in heart: for they shall see God.
> Blessed are the peacemakers: for they shall be called the
> children of God.
> Blessed are they which are persecuted for righteousness' sake:
> for theirs is the kingdom of heaven.
> Blessed are ye, when men shall revile you, and persecute you, and
> shall say all manner of evil against you falsely, for my sake.

This opening salvo contains some of the best-loved language in the New Testament, although the meaning isn't always clear. What does it mean to be poor in spirit? Does this refer to someone who lacks spiritual wealth? Or does it refer to those who, by virtue of empathy, ally themselves with the poor? What does it mean to "inherit the earth" or to be called "the children of God"? Are we not already children of God? Many possibilities for meaning underlie these sayings, inviting us to linger over the phrases, ponder them. They challenge as much as they instruct, which is part of their long-lived power.

Who are these people that Jesus singles out? Those who "mourn" are perhaps those who sense a lack of spiritual growth in those around them, even within themselves. They are those who count their losses. The "meek" are perhaps those who wish to care for and serve others, not only those who step shyly to one side. To "hunger and thirst after righteousness" shows a desire to rise up, to learn about what is good and to come to desire it. The "merciful" are clearly those who love others and show compassion toward them. The "pure in heart" might be those who love what is good and resist whatever is evil, assuming one can figure out the difference. The "peacemakers" are those who refuse to join in with people who sow discord, and instead try to build bridges. Those who are "persecuted for righteousness' sake" refers to those who, acting out of love and care for others, withstand the scorn or punishment of a society that cares little or nothing for such motives.

Here, as everywhere in the scriptures, one has to make adjustments for the fact that these texts came into being thousands of years ago. Meanings of words shift in time, sometimes quite dramatically. And we are dealing with translations of Greek terms that remain difficult to comprehend in their original forms. Even when one does understand the Greek word with some precision, there is the fact that context matters, and one can never read a verse in the Bible without appreciating its place in both the larger narrative and the times during which it was written. Moreover, one must always read the Beatitudes in the context of Judaism. As a devout Jew, Jesus had respect for Mosaic law, even if he wished (as he surely did) to break free from the constraints of an older covenant.

In the Beatitudes, Jesus bestows blessedness on those who behave in particular ways. In Greek the word is *makários*, which also means "delighted" or "happy." Jesus, in effect, lodges a recipe for happiness in these sayings, and his thinking shares key elements with the Eastern idea of karma, a concept central to Hinduism and Buddhism. This idea flowed into Palestine along the Silk Road, a branch of which passed through the village of Capernaum, where Jesus headquartered his ministry. (And one can assume he had contact with all sorts of merchants and travelers, including holy men of one kind or another, who brought teachings from the East.)

Karma defies easy definition, though it is often associated with the notion of rebirth. (The word itself, in Sanskrit, means "deed" or "act.") But its most well-known meaning involves reciprocity. If you are merciful, mercy will be yours. You will reap what you sow. A sense of peace will issue from behaving as a peacemaker. It's a common theme in the teachings of Jesus, but Matthew frames it in a direct way. This form of teaching suggests that Jesus, born in a time of political and religious turbulence, was able to garner the best ideas and reformulate them in unique ways. This was part of his genius, and partly what made him such a memorable teacher. And like all good teachers, Jesus knew his audience.

In this case, it was a rural audience, composed of illiterate farmers, shepherds, tradesmen, fishermen, and the unemployed. Many of them were among the poorest of the poor in Galilee and Judea. So Jesus wisely reached for images and metaphors from the field, from the fishing village and barnyard, for points of illustration—these will mostly be found in the latter parts of the Sermon on the Mount and scattered through the Gospels in parables and sayings. When he says, "I am the vine, ye are my branches," in John 15:5, for example, nobody had to think twice about what he meant, as vineyards formed part of a familiar pastoral landscape. When he compared the kingdom of God to a mustard seed that might spread and grow, everyone understood what he was talking about.

Jesus suggests that living in accordance with his ideas will create a kind of heaven on earth, what he often calls "the kingdom." It's an arresting concept, one that has preoccupied theologians for millennia, although it seems difficult to define with much granularity. Jesus certainly does not mean that the "kingdom" is a physical place, a heaven on earth where all political and religious enemies are vanquished and the righteous live happily forever. I like to think of this as a space that exists outside linear time, an Eternal Now, although I often imagine a gradually realizing kingdom, an awareness of God that comes slowly, that keeps coming, and is never quite resolved but is always moving into clearer spaces.

After the Beatitudes we get a limpid discussion by Jesus of how he regards his new covenant. Of course he doesn't wholly disregard his Judaic roots and context. "Do not imagine that I have come to abolish the Law or the Prophets," he says in Matthew 5:17. He has come, he says, to "fulfill" the law, but there is a sense of completion in fulfillment, a moving beyond the law. He never quite suggests you should forget about the old prophets, but now one must look beyond many of the laws or rethink them in the context of a broader covenant, as he will explain in the six Antitheses, which follow and complete the fifth chapter of Matthew. It's in these that he puts forward his fresh approach, making juxtapositions with the Old Covenant. In most respects, the core of Christian teaching lies in the Antitheses.

Each of the teachings follows a formula: it used to be said that X, but now I say Y. The first one takes up a famous dictum from Mosaic law: thou shalt not kill. But Jesus goes further. He declares, "Anyone who is angry with a brother will answer for it before the court." That is revolutionary, unprecedented. It's not good enough to not murder someone. You should not even get mad at the person. In a sense, the follow-up to this comes in the fifth and six antitheses, which seem to me the most crucial part of Jesus's teachings. In the fifth, he says, "You have heard how it was said: eye for eye and tooth for tooth. But I say this to you: offer no resistance to the wicked." He famously tells his audience to turn the other cheek when struck. In the sixth antithesis, he goes even further: "You have heard how it was said, You will love your neighbor and hate your enemy. But I say this to you: love your enemies and pray for those who persecute you."

G. K. Chesterton once remarked that Christianity would be an effective religion if anybody bothered to try it. Turning the other cheek when struck, even loving your enemies? One can scarcely imagine any political leader taking such a course of action without risking public outcry. Imagine if, after 9/11, George W. Bush had said, "I'm a Christian, so I will not strike back at those who crashed planes into our buildings." What would have been the reaction among his followers in the so-called Bible Belt, of which his home state of Texas is such a large part? But this begs the question at hand: must one resist evil in a nonviolent way? Should Jews have turned the other cheek when Hitler rounded them up? Should the United States have said after Pearl Harbor, "Oh well, too bad" and turned the other cheek to the Japanese imperial forces? One can think of countless circumstances that seemed to have called for violent opposition. Nevertheless, these are the hard teachings of Jesus. They are radical teachings, however difficult to put into effect in the public sphere, although it may well be possible that he was correct, and that even in the above cases the best approach would have been to turn the other cheek, to seek to love those who sought to harm one group or another. We will never know. But the doctrine of passive resistance to evil has inspired a fair number of important figures, including Thoreau, Tolstoy, Gandhi, Martin Luther King, and Nelson Mandela. In the last three cases, these public figures put into practice the theory of nonviolent resistance, and in each case the results were positive.

In any case, Jesus put a teaching before his audience in the Sermon on the Mount that severely tested them. He was a challenging teacher. Working in this radical mode, he makes huge claims for himself, putting forward fierce and new ideas that remain fierce and new, creating what amounts to a New Covenant. Even the symbolic context of the Sermon is relevant here: Jesus speaks from a mountain, as did Moses on Mount Sinai. In doing so, he becomes the new Moses. He asks his listeners to pay attention to the Jewish law, but he also rings changes, modifying the commandments in his own ways, overturning them at certain junctures. He rejects the idea of "an eye for an eye, a tooth for a tooth," which appears in both Deuteronomy 12:21 and Exodus 21:24. That is the old covenant. The new one disallows such primitive and vengeful thinking. (Needless to say, this teaching by Jesus should make it very difficult for serious Christians to support the death penalty.)

Having revised the law, Jesus explains to his followers how they should live and worship. He makes a case for the practice of modesty,

arguing that one should not be seen to be generous, as in giving alms
to the poor in a showy way. "Be careful not to parade your uprightness
in public," he says in Matthew 6:1. In the next passage, he recom-
mends that people should pray alone. "Go to your private room," he
tells his listeners. That is where you will find God, not in the synagogue or Temple. Jesus probably dealt with a lot of hypocritical people
who wished to be seen to be holy, and there is a constant war in the
Gospels with that movement in Judaism known as the Pharisees, an
influential sect who tried to live their religion with a special intensity, attending to the minutiae of the law. But this group probably
attracted hypocrites by the boatload, and it's those who attract the
scorn of Jesus. "Do not imitate the hypocrites," he says frankly in
Matthew 6:5.

Jesus turns to prayer now, putting forward the Lord's Prayer, and it
is still the most widely known prayer in the world, a beautiful expression of humility before God. It begins with praise: "May your name
be held holy" or "Hallowed be thy name." It moves toward submission
to the will of God: "Your will be done." The request for "daily bread"
gives way to repentance, which lies at the heart of the prayer: "And
forgive us our debts, as we forgive those who are in debt to us." Finally,
there is the wish to be kept out of the line of fire: "And do not put us
to the test, but save us from the Adversary." (There are many well-
known translations of this prayer in English, including the classic
King James Version. I often pray in an extemporaneous way, riffing on
the Lord's Prayer. That is, I try to keep vaguely to the form but allow
for creativity with the details.)

The Adversary lives inside each of us, our shadow self. One thinks
of the parable of the weeds and the good grain, which comes in Matthew 13:24–29. In this complex story, the field is sown with good seed
and bad. The Adversary has mingled them. Should one just mow the
whole field, getting rid of everything? No, says Jesus. Wait till the harvest arrives, and let the weeds be sorted out and burned at that mo-

ment. This is a beautiful teaching, and one that relates back to the ending of the Lord's Prayer. That is, in each of us there is the good and bad. In the end there must be sorting. We have an adversarial nature within us, an aspect of our personality that, in Jungian terms, the conscious mind refuses to acknowledge but which still exerts force. It's not that there is good and evil on either side of some great divide. They intermingle. And it's important to let time tell us what we need to know about what is good and what isn't.

Through the sixth chapter of Matthew, Jesus puts forward a plan for a life connected to God in proper ways, telling his listeners not to store up treasures on earth but to dwell on spiritual treasures. "You cannot be the slave both of God and money," he declares in 6:24. This doesn't mean you can't be wealthy: God doesn't keep that kind of ledger. It means you can't spend your time worrying about your bank account, which is the main cause of worry for most of us in a world where money means power, safety, sexual allure, and countless other things. But Jesus is asking for emotional separation between money and self-esteem. In this, he seems very like the Buddha, who didn't disparage wealth but suggested that it should be used only to attain practical ends. He preached (in the *Anguttaranikaya*) the idea of "right livelihood," suggesting that one should acquire material goods by applying one's energies in ethical ways. And he talked about the joy that follows from sharing your wealth with those in need.

The sixth chapter of Matthew closes with the injunction to trust in God, whatever happens. I love and often recall the passage that, in the King James Version, begins: "Consider the lilies of the field, how they grow; they toil not, neither do they spin." Jesus tells the people below him, many of whom lived on the edge of existence, not to worry about food or drink, clothing or shelter. If God takes care to put grass on the fields, clothing them with green, he will take care of you. "Set your hearts on the kingdom first," he says in Matthew 6:33–34. "And do not worry about tomorrow: tomorrow will take care of itself." This is a liberating thought. We have nothing to worry about if we trust in God, in providence, in the beneficent universe that lifts us every day.

Jesus begins the seventh chapter with: "Do not judge, and you will be not judged." This is another crucial teaching, a core element of Christianity, and it's a difficult one. Those who follow the Way of Jesus must not condemn the actions of others. We live in a thoroughly judgmental society, where any crime is attended by a thousand shaming voices, all amplified by social media, which feed on transgressions. Even worse, we tend to judge ourselves harshly. Jesus suggests that God can do the judging himself perfectly well, so leave it to him. If we condemn others, or ourselves, we consign ourselves to judgment in a way that will please no one. Certainly not God.

The end of the Sermon on the Mount moves toward measures of deep reassurance: "Ask, and it will be given you. Search, and you will find; knock, and the door will be opened." These words in Matthew 7:7–8 must have put his listeners at ease, suggesting that prayer is valid, that God is listening. Indeed, a blizzard of wise, unforgettable sayings follows now, moving toward the Golden Rule, the ethic of reciprocity: treat other people in the ways you would wish to be treated. Of course, Jesus didn't invent this idea, which has a long history, going back to the Code of Hammurabi, dating from the eighteenth century BCE. A version of the Golden Rule was even put forward by Rabbi Hillel, a major Jewish teacher and contemporary of Jesus. Almost every religion includes some formulation of this precept, which has proven a sturdy rule of thumb for ethical behavior: do not do something to someone if you wouldn't want that person to do the same thing to you.

The Sermon on the Mount ends with the parable of the house built on solid rock. That is a good house, and it won't easily be dislodged. A house built on sand is less stable, subject to the prevailing winds and rains. We read in Matthew 7:24: "Therefore, everyone who listens to these words of mine and acts on them will be like a sensible man who built his house on rock." A solid foundation for behavior has been laid in these three chapters, where Jesus puts forward in succinct form his basic teachings. We're told by Matthew in a kind of coda: "Jesus had now finished what he wanted to say, and his teaching made a deep impression on the people because he taught them with authority, unlike their own scribes."

Who were these "scribes" who didn't teach with authority, by the way? What were they doing in the company of fishermen and farmers? Jesus may again allude to the Pharisees: fanatics who sought precedents for everything they said in the Hebrew scriptures and adhered to the Law of Moses with a literalness that disturbed Jesus, who certainly taught "with authority." This authority set him apart, and it's why his disciples walked in awe of him, willing to drop everything to assist him as he moved through rural Palestine as a rabbi, gathering his wisdom into words, teaching in ways that have meant so much to his followers for more than twenty centuries. It's an authority that derives from deep in the self, where that spark of the kingdom will always be found.

Emerson put the matter succinctly in his "Divinity School Address" in 1838, and it seems to me relevant to my reading of the Sermon on the Mount:

> Jesus Christ belonged to the true race of the prophets. He saw with open eye the mystery of the soul. Drawn by its severe harmony, ravished with its beauty, he lived in it, and had his being there. Alone in all history he estimated the greatness of man. One man was true to what is in you and me. He saw that God incarnates himself in man, and evermore goes forth anew to take possession of his World. He said, in this jubilee of sublime emotion, "I am divine. Through me, God acts; through me, speaks. Would you see God, see me."

▪ TOWARD A COMMUNITY OF FAITH:
RESURRECTION THINKING

Our life is a fire dampened, or as a fire shut up in stone. Dear children,
it must blaze, and not remain smoldering, smothered.
—*Jacob Boehme*, De Incarnatione Verbi

The last thing to be realized is the incarnation.
—*Norman O. Brown*, Love's Body

It's important to emphasize the goal of Christianity, which is not resurrection but what I would call Resurrection Thinking. This, for me,
involves getting away from the literal-mindedness that has too often
sunk Christians, miring them in a kind of thought that resists the
multiplicity and many-layered consciousness that symbolic thinking not only allows but creates. As in the first epigraph above, from
Boehme, I would argue that our real life, our life in God, lies hidden,
smothered by the weight of rational thought in the secular world and
by the heaviness of literal thought within the Christian world, where
the letter and not the spirit of the Word are honored, and where the
scriptures themselves become a fetishized object, worshipped in itself, to the detriment of the spirit. In Paul's letter to the Colossians
(3:3–4), we are told that "your life is now hidden with Christ" but that
when Christ reappears, "you will also appear with him in glory."

This reappearance does not happen tomorrow. It is always present.

We are like the Phoenix of myth, perpetually being reborn from
our ashes. And he who is "not busy being born is busy dying," as Bob
Dylan sang. The Way of Jesus leads to perpetual rebirth, a renaissance on every level, with the Resurrection happening now, without
limits.

This mode of thinking is specifically Christian. The New Testament reshaped the Old Testament, just as Jesus refigured the Old
Covenant, proposing a New Covenant wherein the rigid Deuteron-

omistic stranglehold is broken, so that a kind of postlegalistic wildness appears, not anarchy but a spirit-filled wildness symbolized by the Pentecostal tongues of fire that appeared over the heads of the disciples of Jesus after his death, thus signaling the coming of the Holy Spirit. Resurrection Thinking invites, as Jesus said, a fulfillment of the Old Covenant, however, not its abolition, as in Matthew 5:17: "I did not come to abolish but to fulfill the law." But what does this mean, fulfillment?

To a degree, it's about making the historical unconscious conscious, bringing shadowy realities into the brightness of daily life. It's about understanding the myths in the Old Testament as luminous parallels, not just prefiguration—an archetype that demands renewal, alertness to the contours of meaning, its radiance. As Norman O. Brown writes: "Nothing happens for the first time. There is nothing in the Old Testament which does not recur in the New Testament. This is the *concordia scripturarum*, the mysterious correspondence between the two scriptures, to be seen by those who have eyes to see."[23] And so Jacob wrestling with his angel is not unlike Jesus wrestling with the Adversary. The sacrifice of Isaac, who is pictured as Abraham's "only son" in Genesis 22:2, doesn't just prefigure the sacrifice of God's "only son" in Jesus—it's a looking glass, and we step through it to the other side, into a genuine understanding of God's love as a father's love for his son: without limit. And so when we see God in familial bonds, we understand that love bathes our life and redeems it.

This is the "redemption" of the Messiah, as we hear from Jesus himself in the suggestive fifth chapter of John: "You search the scriptures because you believe that in them you will find eternity. It is these scriptures that testify about me, but you seem unwilling to come to me for life." Jesus is thinking about the Old Testament here, of course, as the New Testament didn't exist yet. "If you believed in Moses, you would believe in me, for he wrote about me," he says, in what remains a cryptic but suggestive assertion. In this way Jesus invites us to read New into the Old, to understand that before Abraham "was," Jesus "is"—a rupturing of syntax that indicates the rupture of time.

This is Resurrection Thinking: a willing submission to the symbolic meanings of scriptures, an awareness that reading the Word means reading beyond the idolatry of literal-minded interpretation, allowing for many levels of resonance and symbolic complexity, as symbols are by their very nature open-ended. "Behold, I make all things new," says the Almighty seated on the throne of heaven in Revelation 5:5. Making it new means cracking the literal surface of the stories, opening them up to crackling-fresh life.

Without a growing sense of the Resurrection, one misses out on one of the primary experiences that being human affords: a call to renewal and a connection to the infinite within us, which I call God but which may, of course, have many names. What I call Resurrection Thinking works on multiple levels, helping the individual to deepen his or her sense of reality while, in a larger sense, ushering forward the so-called Kingdom of God, which necessarily involves a community of faith, and which begins in the present moment, with the body, living among neighbors whom you treat as you would like to be treated, with compassion.

The Way of Jesus invites us to think again about how we want to or ought to live our lives, although it's worth pondering what the "Jesus" element adds. In the early decades of the first century, there were other "ways" that attracted attention, meaning religious paths and practices. A revealing passage occurs in Acts 12:24: "Now a certain Jew named Apollos, born in Alexandria, an eloquent man with a strong knowledge of the scriptures, came to Ephesus. This man had been instructed in the Way of God, and being fervent in spirit, he spoke and taught accurately the things of the Lord, though he knew only the baptism of John." He didn't know about Jesus, and yet he seemed in possession of important knowledge and skills. As it was, some Christian women soon took him aside and explained that Jesus had amplified the message of the Way, and he quickly adopted these teachings, becoming an early evangelist.

So what did having a knowledge of the teachings of Jesus really add to what Apollos already knew?

It added the Incarnation. Christianity is above all else an incarnational religion, based on historical contingency, connected to a specific era and place when God entered time and space in the form of this man, Jesus, who represents a "putting into flesh," or incarnation, of the spirit. A paradox here needs elaboration. Jesus is the Word, the *logos*: he was before and after time. And so the Christ story is about what happens when God enters literal time to break us free from its bonds. "Only through time," says Eliot in *Burnt Norton*, "time is conquered," and this is how God gets us out of the fix of clock time, liberates us from the cycle of seasons. It allows us to say with John Donne: "Death be not proud."

The Way of Jesus encourages us to see where and how God happens by direct experience of his death and resurrection. As Rowan Williams writes in *The Wound of Knowledge*, "The Spirit's work is to make the believer like Christ, and being like Christ means living through certain kinds of human experience—not once, but daily."[24] This "living through" means experiencing fully the inevitable suffering that is part of human experience and which forms the basis for transformation—the widening of consciousness embodied in that Greek word *metanoia*: opening the mind to the wider mind of God. This is, in fact, the kind of transfiguration that Jesus modeled and invites.

In Paul's stirring second letter to the Corinthians, he talks about the daily rejections and afflictions that are simply part of being human, the daily dying through which the spirit works its magic, which Paul frames as a transformation from "one degree of glory to another" (2 Corinthians 3:18). Paul certainly didn't imagine this as a one-off change, as in being "born again," once and forever. He envisioned a perpetual rebirth, which means finding the everlasting God within us, as suggested in Genesis 1:27, where we are told that we were cre-ated "in the image and likeness of God." This is what it means to get back to the garden, back to the life source that bubbles up in each human being. Jesus does, in symbolic fashion, restore us: the sins of Adam and Eve are forgiven once and for all, and we inhabit again our timeless bodies, even while still caught in the flesh of ordinary time.

The incarnational aspect of Resurrection Thinking can't be overemphasized. The soul desperately needs the body, which is the medium of its production. *Hoc est corpus*: "This is my body." As the visionary poet William Blake wrote in *The Marriage of Heaven and Hell*: "Man has no Body distinct from his Soul for that called Body is a portion of Soul discerned by the five Senses." At a stroke, Blake dissolves the classic bifurcation of mind versus body or material world versus spiritual world. He does so by seeing the Old and New as one, a simultaneity of experience in which history becomes poetry: a series of images that we can dwell on, which fill us with delight and open our consciousness, so that "before" and "after" collapse into *now*. Lin-ear history dies, much as the Phoenix dies and is reborn from the ashes, much as Jesus dies and we, in imitation, die and become Christ, taking on the "mind of Christ," in Paul's lovely formulation.

Blake, in another memorable poem, begs God to keep human be-ings "from single vision and Newton's sleep." Newton, of course, was his great contemporary, the physicist who studied the world in mate-rial terms. Blake argues against the "single vision" that pervades the scientific way of knowledge by measurement and verification. Blake regarded this as a form of literal-mindedness, and he suggests that we think poetically, symbolically, with double or triple or fourfold vision, refusing to allow the letter of the law to kill us. As Paul writes in 2 Corinthians 3:6: "God has enabled us to be competent advocates of the New Covenant, not possessed by the letter but the spirit of the law; for the law kills, but the spirit gives life."

The Way of Jesus moves inexorably toward transformation or resurrection on some level. "All faith is resurrection faith," says

Balthasar, as noted above, and this remark embodies the conviction that whatever has been dead may come alive again, transmogrified in ways that can't be understood while living under the opaque veil of faithlessness, with a lack of trust in providence, caught in Blake's "single vision." But "faith" is one of those ferociously difficult terms to define. It sounds wishy-washy, a generic term that isn't easily translated into hard experience. To be frank, I've never quite understood the oft-quoted definition of faith as "the substance of things hoped for, the evidence of things not seen" (Hebrews 11:1). Resurrection Thinking moves away from hoping for anything. It means living the truth of Jesus, his continuous emergence, and the realities of a gradually realizing kingdom.

Gadamer nicely describes faith as "a process of correction"[25] in which our sense of self in relation to reality undergoes continual revision as it moves toward understanding or awareness while brushing against the logos—the deep and organizing spiritual knowledge at the core of experience. Gadamer argues, with passion, that each of us is "historically-effected," and that we can't break free of either our own deep prejudices or the time in which we live, which has its own transitory but firmly held convictions about the nature of reality; but he doesn't see this as a bad thing, just something we must take into account as we proceed. He criticizes Enlightenment thinkers who imagined they could separate themselves from prejudice and subjectivity, acquiring neutrality and bowing to the world of nature, with its universal laws. Gadamer dismisses such an outlook as fanciful, regarding the interpretation of experience as inevitably a process involved in community, in a community of interpretation, or what I would call a "faith community."

Resurrection Thinking, as envisioned by the Way of Jesus, opens possibilities for freedom, for "enlightenment," within the context of a beloved community. This freedom is difficult to find in a wholly secular world, where many of the doors of spiritual perception are locked or seem not even to exist. Jesus repeatedly invites participation in a wider consciousness and symbolic revision as well as rebirth, and so—as Christians—we see history not as individual and wholly separate moments but as a glorious whole, a fusion of inner and outer realities, a melding of past and future into the fiery present. The Messiah inspires this unification, when the mind and body rise together in full appreciation of what love can really do when unlocked, implemented, turned into a way of being. This is the kind of Resurrection Thinking framed by Thomas Traherne, the seventeenth-century mystic and poet, who wrote in *Centuries of Meditations*: "You never enjoy the world aright till the sea itself flows in your veins, till you are clothed with the heavens and crowned with the stars; and perceive yourself to be the sole heir of the whole world, and more than so, because men are in it who are everyone sole heirs as well as you. Till you can sing and rejoice and delight in God, as misers do in gold, and kings in scepters, you can never enjoy the world."

THREE

THE CHURCH YEAR

Live in each season as it passes; breathe the air, drink the drink,
taste the fruit, and resign yourself to the influence of the earth.
—*Thoreau,* Journals

He has balanced the love of change in them by a love of permanence.
He has contrived to gratify both tastes together in the very real
world He has made, by that union of change and permanence, which
we call Rhythm. He gives them the seasons, each season different
yet every year the same, so that spring is always felt as a novelty yet
always as the recurrence of an immemorial theme. He gives them
in his Church a spiritual year; they change from a fast to a feast,
but it is the same feast as before.
—*C. S. Lewis,* The Screwtape Letters

The Church Year is a calendar that mediates our sense of the unfolding liturgical seasons, allowing us to think and feel our way into the
contours of sacred time. It is deeply about practice, offering points
along the calendar for reflection on the life of Jesus and occasions for
action, allowing our personal life rhythms to connect to larger spiritual rhythms as experienced by the community of faith. One might
see the year as a gift, one that allows us to reshape ourselves, to be

transformed gradually in the course of Advent, Lent, Easter, and—that lovely phrase—Ordinary Time. I know that the progression through the months and symbolic phases of the Church Year have affected me deeply, form a kind of objective correlative or series of correspondences that lift me out of my personal life, its joys and griefs, connecting me to larger patterns that help to explain and externalize in a public way my own feelings and thoughts.

■ ADVENT TO CHRISTMAS

The Church Year begins with Advent, which means "coming" or "emergence." It's another version of a wonderful Greek word, *parousia*—which might also be translated as "miraculous appearance" or "manifestation," and which often arises in Christian discourse. The four Sundays of Advent—an intense and beautiful period of anticipation—lead up to Christmas itself, the season's high point, culminating in the arrival of the Son of God, Jesus, who has made himself "incarnate," thoroughly embodied, given flesh. God's spiritual presence arises within us slowly through Advent, symbolized by the miracle—or myth—of the Virgin Birth, when a young woman becomes pregnant with God's own son.

I don't worry about the fantastic nature of this pregnancy. Mythical tales about unions between human beings and gods reach back to the ancient Egyptians, Greeks, and earlier. One thinks of Amenkept, for instance: the pharaoh who built Luxor on the Nile. If you've been there, you've seen the glistening images on the walls: the angel announcing to the Virgin Queen that she will bear a child, the miraculous conception (which included the virgin holding a cross to her lips as a sign of life—a traditional symbol, unrelated to Christianity). The symbolism of a Virgin Birth is familiar to anyone who has studied world mythology. Joseph Campbell observes: "On the level simply of legend, without regard to the possibility of an actual miracle, the

Virgin Birth must be interpreted as a mythic motif from the Persian or Greek, not Hebrew, side of the Christian heritage; and in the two recorded versions of the Nativity scene, more motifs appear from this gentilic side."[1]

Christian myth inhabits and transforms the elements in this mythic material, as in the Christmas story, a tale of origins that allows us to celebrate the coming of Jesus in this season of expectation, as we wait through the four weeks before Christmas for the manifestation of God's gift to us, as symbolized by the Advent wreath—four purple candles set in a ring of evergreens, with a single white candle in the middle. We light one (suggesting penitence) candle a week until the fourth Sunday, when the candle is sometimes red to symbolize joy. Christmas Eve—the night before Christmas itself—we light the "Christ candle," which is white, for purity and innocence. The circle, of course, is a symbol of eternal time, or timeless time. Needless to say, this arrangement of candles suggests the four points of a cross as well: a subtle gesture toward the Crucifixion, which lies in the distant future. "The light shines in darkness," the gospel writer says in John 1:5.

The season of Christmas means a great deal to me and to all who follow the Way of Jesus. In my own life, I feel a deep and lovely sense of anticipation, one that goes back to my childhood in Pennsylvania. In those days, I was thinking about the presents that might appear under the tree on Christmas morning, about the colorful lights strung on houses in my neighborhood, about the carols I would hear. Today I think about how miraculous this story remains: the radical notion that God would become man so that man could become God. It's a personal story, a family story: and so I connect to it in my adulthood on many levels, and it brings me closer to my own nuclear family. (I've got three sons, and Christmas always reminds me of the day each of them was born, and how much life they have brought into my own experience of being human.)

In so many ways, I tend to agree with Richard Rohr that "Christmas is more significant than Easter. Christmas is already Easter!"[2]

The idea here is that since God chose to become a human, we're already "saved." God didn't need to sacrifice his son to "save" anyone: "Christ was Plan A," says Rohr, "not Plan B." Atonement in its more puritanical inflections implies "that God had a plan, we messed it up, and then God had to come back in to mop up our mistakes." He refers to the thirteenth-century Franciscan John Duns Scotus, who believed that God's purpose from the beginning was to use Jesus to reveal Godself, the Christ in each of us. This idea makes Christmas, the Advent of God in the world, so crucial to Christian living and spirituality. We're already there: enlightened. We only need to discover the remarkable dimensions of the kingdom already growing inside us.

The story of the Way of Jesus is the story of Incarnation, the interjection of Christ into the world, so that human beings could begin to comprehend the mystery of God by seeing how he talked and walked, how he behaved among his neighbors, related to his friends, prayed without ceasing, and met the pain of his own mortality with grace and wisdom. He modeled suffering, opening a path to redemption and at-one-ment with God. He taught us how to love God, the meaning of faith itself, which is trust in God. Perhaps most crucially, he taught us about renewal as resurrection.

It's not surprising that early Christians began to cast about for information about the origins of Jesus, needing to think about the Incarnation in a narrative way. It's clear from the letters of Paul that the burgeoning church in the first century knew nothing of Christmas: as noted earlier, Paul never mentions Joseph, the manger in Bethlehem, or anything we traditionally associate with this sacred holiday, which Christians didn't even begin to celebrate until early in the fourth century (partly because birthdays didn't really matter to most people in those days and partly because nobody had any idea when exactly Jesus was born). Certainly Mark and John knew nothing of Jesus's birth, and had no interest in its circumstances. It was left to Matthew and Luke to gather this material—which may have already been in circulation—into the larger narrative of Jesus, giving him a family, earthly parents, and a tale of beginnings that people could understand. They clearly drew on different sources. The two versions of Christmas aren't easily reconciled and suggest wildly different traditions. Matthew begins with a genealogy of Jesus that starts with Abraham and runs through King David: a distinctly Jewish heritage, which suggests something about his original audience. By contrast, Luke speaks mainly to Gentiles, and he begins with Adam, thus downplaying the Jewish angle. David remains a pivotal figure in both genealogies, however, thus fulfilling an ancient prophecy that the Messiah would have Davidic origins, as in Jeremiah 23:5–6: "I will raise to David a branch of righteousness; a King shall reign and prosper, and execute judgment and righteousness in the earth." One has to adjust to the fact of these different stories.

I actually like having two versions, as it reminds me that one can't settle on any version of Jesus; the Christmas tales invite mythic interpretations. This isn't history, it's mystery, and each story summons strong but different emotions. The account in Matthew is frightening, with Jesus being chased out of Judea by the wicked King Herod, who wants to kill him because of the rumors about a new king he has heard from the magi, or "wise men," from the East. Herod issues a decree that all children under the age of two should be murdered, so that no rival king will have a chance to thrive: the so-called Massacre of the Innocents, so brutally depicted by the painter Rubens in 1612. It's a tale of horror, one that involves Jesus being whisked away to Egypt for safety, where he and his family hide out until the danger has passed—the parallels between Jesus and Joseph in the Old Testament have been widely noted, and they remain striking. As ever, the idea that Jesus fulfills or replicates earlier prophecies and patterns was intentionally played out by the Gospel writers.

In Luke we get a much softer, even genial version of Christmas: shepherds keeping watch over their flocks by night, a starry canopy overhead. It's a peaceful scene in the manger in Bethlehem, with no threat of children under the age of two being murdered, with no flight to Egypt. Indeed, the Lukan birth story ends with Jesus being taken to the Temple in Jerusalem to be circumcised on the eighth day, in keeping with Jewish custom. In this version one gets lovely complementary stories of Simeon, the old man who had waited so long to see the Messiah, and Anna, a prophet, who has also waited a long time for the child who would mark "the redemption of Jerusalem." Luke's Christmas story ends with the flourish of a good novelist: "And the child grew and waxed strong in spirit: he was filled with wisdom, and the grace of God was upon him" (Luke 2:40).

The idea of the Virgin Birth is central to the Christmas story, and it's been widely viewed as theologically suggestive: one of the mysteries, worthy of awe and contemplation. Yet it's not an idea developed in any substantial way in the Gospels, where there is little in the way of interpretation. The brief passages in Matthew and Luke refer back to a verse in the Hebrew scriptures (Isaiah 7:14), more or less repeating earlier passages: "Therefore the Lord will give you a sign: the young maiden will give birth to a son, and he will be called Immanuel." (The Hebrew word *almah*, meaning "young woman," is without any virginal connotations. That was a later twist, as the term passed into Greek.)

The idea of the Virgin Birth nonetheless has mythic power, and one need not dwell on the literal truth. That would be pointless, in my understanding of how mythic truth operates. Think about it like this: God inhabits a special person, in the form of Jesus, who is endowed with godlike qualities. He is a man so identified with the "mind of Christ," as Paul says, that he truly becomes God, and he shows us how to access this power. We all become children of God under his aegis. That is, we connect to what is often called the Cosmic Christ, the eternal spirit of God as manifested in the world, and identified in the Christian tradition as Jesus of Nazareth.

Christmas is very much about Mary as well as Jesus, and it turns us lovingly toward our own mothers and the mystery of our own souls being "incarnate," turned into flesh, manifested. The figure of Mary, as an object of contemplation, allows us to access what Jung calls the anima as well as the animus in our souls (I like the word "soul" as a translation of the Greek word *psyche*), as well as in God. These gendered terms are "images" that we carry in our unconscious, each being a "hereditary factor of primordial origin engraved in the living organic system" of each human being, part of our "inherited system of psychic adaptation."[3] The idea that God is both male and female is striking as well as useful. I often feel—for one reason or another—more like accessing the anima image, as in Mary: she is a comforting presence, serene and courageous, especially in how she deals with the terror of her situation, exhibiting what Hemingway called "grace under pressure." She found divine support in her moment of need: "And the angel came in to visit her, and said, Hail, you that are highly favored, the Lord is with you: blessed are you among women" (Luke 1:38). Her generous presence—largely a matter of projection, since we don't really get much feeling for her personality in the Gospels—dominates the Christmas season, and it's no surprise that artists have been drawn to her, attempting with considerable success to capture her aura (although it should also be remembered that Mary was not so keen on the idea that her son, at thirty, chose to become an itinerant healer. One reads about her and Jesus's brothers trying to bring him home in the third chapter of Mark. "He has lost his senses," they say, although we don't actually know whether Mary or one of his brothers said this).

To inhabit the expectancy of Advent, taking pleasure in the textures of the Christmas season, with the cold weather and shortening days, it's useful to let fearfulness and an expectancy of joy mingle. The "bleak midwinter," as formulated in the hymn, is a dark time. But as the poet Theodore Roethke says: "In a dark time the eye begins to see." Perhaps we begin to see most clearly on the darkest nights, as the light barely peeps through the holes in the black sky. We wait and wait for dawn. The idea of waiting, of course, is wholly human, part of our natural fragility, our "just passing through" anxieties as we inhabit our lives. Indeed, aren't we always anticipating something, and don't we have to learn to embrace, not dislike, this uncertainty?

The weeks of Advent bring us close to the experience of waiting, hoping, dreaming. The practical sides of the coming holiday may overwhelm us, and do at times seem trivial; we may recoil from the noise of commerce, which is unbearable as the season unfolds, with secular trappings of Christmas that overwhelm us, making it difficult to focus on the liturgical season. Yet the child in us waits with hope for something good: a few lively meals with family and friends, perhaps some happy times in church. But I find in this anticipation a feeling of dread as well. The sense of impending darkness, one that could obliterate us, can overwhelm or, at least, oppress us. It's not surprising that many who suffer from depression find Advent, and the season of Christmas itself, unbearable. Some feel cut off from the sources of light, with a vague feeling of homelessness, of missing friends and relatives, or being apart from them at a time when everyone else, it seems, tilts homeward. This season is, as much as anything, a time of grieving, as one confronts the ghosts of Christmases past, which inevitably bring up losses. It's not for nothing that we talk about "the dead of winter." The season has its sorrows, although the Christmas moment is a moment of light in darkness. That December 25 wasn't the day when Jesus was "really" born does not matter. Matthew and Luke never specify a date for his birth—the calendar would not have matched ours in any case. Christmas falls on the final day of the Roman Saturnalia, and it relates to the winter solstice as well, that astrological moment marking the longest night of the year, which also becomes a turning point; it gestures toward longer hours of light, an awakening world. The Roman emperor Aurelian marked this as a feast day meant to celebrate the birth of the Unconquered Sun (*Sol Invictus*), which suggests that this day near the end of December already signaled triumph.

As it were, the darkness has become oppressive by the time the

Christ child enters the world, so he becomes a symbol of light over-coming darkness, as put conclusively in John: "I am the light of the world!" (John 8:12).

In a small church in London a few years ago, in the borough of Islington on Christmas Eve, I attended a service in which an elderly priest read the opening of John in a sonorous voice, his words almost pinging off the ancient stone walls. It struck me forcefully that this hymn to *logos*, or "the Word," is profoundly relevant at Christmas: "In the beginning was the Word, and the Word was with God, and the Word was God. The same was in the beginning with God. All things were made by him, and without him was not anything made that was made. In him was life; and the life was the light of men. And the light shined in darkness; and the darkness understood it not."

So Jesus—the Messiah or Cosmic Christ—represents an em-bodiment, the putting on of flesh in the act of Incarnation. God as *logos*—such a difficult term to define or comprehend—becomes (in my thinking at least) the comprehending feature of the universe, an active and conscious presence in an otherwise unconscious world. *Logos* (Christ or Word) was there with God in the beginning and will remain in the end, and so it becomes something different from Jesus, who nevertheless embodied this idea. Among many other things, *logos* is light as well: it shines in the dark, even though the dark has no idea about what is going on. By "following" Jesus we con-nect to the Christ in him and through him, moving toward God, uniting with the divine that was present before presence itself. I often think of Eliot's depiction of Christ as *logos* or "the Word" in "Geron-tion," where he recalls "The word within a word, unable to speak a word, / Swaddled in darkness."

However complex, even paradoxical, the idea of *logos* may seem, the ritual of Christmas has an appealing simplicity and invites con-templation as one approaches the manger on Christmas Eve, a happy moment in the Church Year, often celebrated with candlelight ser-vices, special music, pageants, and liturgies that include readings of biblical passages or poems and traditional music, a service called "lessons and carols." The idea that Jesus was born at night is reflected in hymns, such as "Silent Night, Holy Night." (Whenever possible, you should listen at this time of year to Bach's great *Christmas Oratorio*, with a spirit of joy and expectation in the key of D major; notice in particular the famous "Pastorale," in which the piping of shepherds is played on the oboe to stunning effect.)

The moment of incarnation represents the humanization of an abstruse theological point. And so *logos* becomes a tiny child in a manger. One can relate to any child, especially an infant. The human family understands the strangeness of birth, an event in which creatures utterly distinct from their parents come into being, are loved and shaped by those around them, and (in best-case scenarios) join hands with the larger community in the great dance. If all we had was the opening verses of John's Gospel, we might not feel as connected to Jesus as we do. But the spectacle of incarnation changes everything: we have each of us been there. We understand the vulnerability of the child. We "identify," sympathize. And it doesn't require a massive effort to imagine what it felt like for Mary and Joseph as they wandered in Judea, away from their home village of Nazareth, looking for a place to stay.

By the simple fact of his birth in a barn in the middle of nowhere special, Jesus qualifies as an outsider, a child on the margins. His father was apparently a working man, or *tekton*, not a wealthy landowner, merchant, or public official. Indeed, the obscurity of Jesus's birth seems absolutely necessary as a means to advance his story and its larger meaning. His innocence and vulnerability, his lack of wealth and position in society: these only add to his profile, and teach us that we don't need wealth or position to gain enlightenment. The teachings of Jesus, as with the illustrations of his life as shaped by the Gospel writers, suggest that the poor will inherit the earth, that the last shall be first. He was a lowly man, a rural man, who spoke to those at the ragged edges. And what he said changed everything.

Shortly after the birth, the magi arrive, these wise men from the East who come to pay homage, seeking the light; in the *mythos* it's important that they follow a star, a mysterious and especially bright star that hovers above the manger. This is one of those moments called an epiphany, the term signifying a manifestation of truth, a sudden pouring forth of divine reality. January 6 is the usual date for celebrating this feast of recognition, and it's been written about often. I tried my own hand at expressing the intense emotion that gathers around this image in "Magi":

> In the iron winter days
> we sense them moving on bare hills
> like inklings, omens:
> wise ones coming from afar
> with eager sun-dried faces
> under heavy brows,
> their curiosity a thing of wonder.
>
> They've been riding hard for months
> on lumpy camels,
> with a growing certainty that's patience
> magnified by faith in what will come,
> now fixing on a star
> that hovers in their brains
> above a barn, far out of sight.
>
> Our prayers have failed us,
> so we listen as we wait for them,
> this company of allies, aids
> on this blue-bleak midwinter
> where—in silence we have not imagined,
> in its frost of solitude—
> they will find us waiting:

For the desert wisdom of their coming.
For their slice of light on sand,
the purple shadows and the scent of grapes,
the blood-bright juice
that brings us faithfully again together
in this room of need, where
surely they find us—kneeling, still.

As a child, the thought of "three kings" coming from the East intrigued me. As an adult, I think of the magi within us and the resources of desert wisdom. We take this with us into the room where we pray, into the church sanctuary, or wherever we go with a hope of sustenance or inspiration, an expectation of transcendence. The magi represent this journeying toward the light, with their doggedness and hope.

The sole account of these magi, in Matthew, doesn't number these unlikely visitors, whose visit recalls a prophecy found in Isaiah 60:3: "And the gentiles shall come to thy light, and kings to the brightness of thy rising." They may be magicians, sorcerers, or astrologers. The tradition of three "kings" reaches back to the third century in Egypt, where they eventually acquired names: Caspar, Melchior, and Balthasar. That marvelous English monk, the Venerable Bede, suggested that the three kings represented three parts of the known world: Europe, Asia, and Africa. And so one has become used to various manifestations of the magi, often with varying skin colors. "We three kings of Orient are," or so begins the legendary hymn of 1857, a staple of the season. They bring gifts of gold, frankincense, and myrrh: each of them a radiant symbol. Gold, then as now, was deeply prized; frankincense was a perfume used in temple rituals; myrrh was "the finest of spices," a precious oil used for ceremonies, such as the anointment of kings and priests, as noted in Exodus 30:23.

There are several weeks in the post-Christmas phase of Epiphany, a time that celebrates the growing light, a symbol of the gift of Jesus to

the world. This phase marks, in theory, a return to Ordinary Time—
that suggestive phrase attached to parts of the Church Year that are
not hugely laden with meaning. But there is a lull here, a contemplative if anxious space that everyone who follows the Way of Jesus
will appreciate. It's a time when we go back to what Auden in "For
the Time Being" describes aptly as a difficult period. "The Christmas
Feast is almost fading in memory," he writes. And yet, "To those who
have seen / The Child, however dimly, however incredulously, / The
Time Being is, in a sense, the most trying time of all." Having seen
the light emerge from a dark period, one rubs one's eyes, wondering
how to assimilate the Word. It's so dark out, one wonders if the year
has in fact turned toward the light, as promised by the calendar.

Depending on one's tradition, the five to nine Sundays after
Christmas (the calendar plays a role here) offer a time to focus on
what it meant for Jesus to enter the world, to begin his ministry at
the age of thirty, walking in Galilee and showing us how to live according to the Way. Before stepping out on the road, he wrestled with
Satan in the Judean desert for forty days. During his ministry, he baptized followers in rivers or lakes, as he was himself baptized by John
the Baptist. He moved among the poor, among beggars, lepers, and
whores, and spoke to them about his ideas, as in the Sermon on the
Mount. This was Ordinary Time for him, although it was hardly ordinary. And his example challenges us, living in the weeks after Christmas, to think how to utilize the light that has emerged.

To follow him, we should work for change, moving expectantly
among the dispossessed or marginalized, however uncomfortable this
makes us, however impossible the task may at times seem. To practice
what Jesus preached, we must turn the other cheek, love our neighbors as ourselves, and pray as often as we can. As Paul wrote to the
church in Thessalonica: "Rejoice always, pray without ceasing, give
thanks in all circumstances, for this is the will of God in Christ Jesus
for you" (1 Thessalonians 5:16–18). I think the difficulties of imitating Jesus here go without saying: it's not easy. I have struggled over

the years with loving my enemies, or those I perhaps only conceive of as "enemies." My own experience is that listening is the hard work of the Way, really listening, trying to absorb what people are saying without getting defensive. It's often humiliating and anxiety-making, of course.

I've been lucky in that my work, as a writer and teacher, has taken me into the world. After the 2003 US invasion of Iraq, for instance, I traveled often to the Middle East, giving talks or meeting with writers and teachers in Jordan, in Egypt, in Israel, Morocco, and elsewhere. My own outrage over this brutal invasion fed my anger: I could barely tolerate the idea of a hundred thousand or more innocents, women and children included, killed in order to prosecute our "war of choice." I was too quick, however, to demonize those who disagreed with me, and prayed many times before talking in public about the war, trying to keep my sense of openness to the experience of others, possibly to understand their viewpoint. I didn't succeed, but I tried, and I will keep trying—even now as the consequences of this invasion continue to multiply, yielding bitter fruit for the people of this sad region.

Politics is often problematic for me, a source of discouragement or fury. During the Vietnam War era, I found myself befuddled and enraged by American actions. The assassination of Martin Luther King Jr. proved a very hard time for me, as it did for the nation. I've often felt helpless in the face of national or world events, and I rely on my prayer life, my study of the Bible, my commitment to the liturgies in the course of the Church Year, to shape my responses. Indeed, reading the Psalms is always a fine way for me to adjust, emotionally and spiritually, to upheavals in my life: this cycle of hymns touches on every human feeling, from blind rage to befuddlement, from awe to celebration. It's no wonder they have found a central place in every Christian service throughout the year.

The liturgy of epiphany moves toward readjustment, toward renewal and refreshment. Indeed, the idea of epiphany itself, which involves a sudden awareness of deeper truth and transformation, seems to me at the heart of Christian thinking. Thomas Merton's admirable reflection on his "Fourth and Walnut Epiphany" bears mentioning here. In the piece, he talks about being seized unexpectedly by insight one day in Louisville, Kentucky. Here is an abbreviated version of that passage:

> In Louisville, at the corner of Fourth and Walnut, in the center of the shopping district, I was suddenly overwhelmed with the realization that I loved all those people, that they were mine and I theirs, that we could not be alien to one another even though we were total strangers. It was like waking from a dream of separateness, of spurious self-isolation in a special world, the world of renunciation and supposed holiness. The whole illusion of a separate holy existence is a dream.[4]

Would that we could all experience epiphanies like this, times when we understood our connection to others instead of wallowing in our separateness, in being angry with our neighbors, or those in political power. The Christmas season, in its extension from the first week of Advent through the Feast of the Epiphany, brings us wonderfully together as the Body of Christ, as a community based on trust in God. And, with luck, we move into the world to create community in any way we can.

▪ LENT

All four Gospels devote a substantial part of their narratives to the Easter story, which coincides with Passover, when large numbers of devout Jews every year made their way from various parts of Palestine to the holy city and the Temple itself. As we read in Luke 9:51: "When the days drew close for him to be taken up, he set his face toward Jerusalem." As followers of the Way, we set ourselves each year on a similar journey, with the intention to move through penitence to the joy of the Resurrection in Easter. But this waiting time, a kind of parallel to Advent, only more severe, given its culmination, is Lent, after a Saxon word meaning "length" but also deriving from *lencton*, the Old English word for "lengthen," which presumably refers to the lengthening days of spring.

The liturgical year tracks the seasons, with early spring being a period of exasperated waiting for the warmth, a few months that can be hard to bear, especially if you live in a cold northern climate as I have, where this particular season has severe ups and downs, at times sunk in the depths of freezing winter, though with sudden glimpses of bright and bitter light. The Lenten season properly begins with Ash Wednesday and ends, about six weeks later, with Easter itself. These forty days in the wilderness are akin to the time Jesus spent in the desert as he prepared for his ministry (analogous to the forty years during which the Israelites wandered in the desert in search of the Promised Land). It's a period calling for repentance and penance, marked by prayers seeking forgiveness and by fasting.

There is a cleansing aspect to Ash Wednesday. It's a day of penitence, when one attends a special service during which the priest "imposes" a cross of ashes on your forehead, often saying this phrase: "Remember that you are dust, and to dust you shall return." The service itself is haunting, often featuring a recitation of Psalm 51, which opens: "Have mercy on me, O God, according to thy lovingkindness: according unto the multitude of thy tender mercies, blot out my transgressions." Confession is the marrow of this service, a move central to all efforts to live according to the Way. One needs a clean heart to worship God, and there is deep freedom here. I find myself moved in almost any weekly service by the recitation of the confession, asking forgiveness for "the things I have done, the things I have left undone."

There are so many ways to confess our sins, but these mainly center on our failure to love our neighbors as ourselves. It is so hard to do this, and often seems impossible: a mad quest. We even fail to treat ourselves very well! Yet there is much to be gained by dwelling in quiet on our waywardness, our errors, the memories of which weigh on us. We ask God to release us from this burden, allowing us to walk out into the world in a fresh way, forgiving others as we forgive ourselves.

But self-abnegation—hating our flesh, our sinfulness—is self-defeating. I have little time for the severities of the Calvinist tradition, with its tendency to dwell on human wickedness. I refer to John Calvin, the sixteenth-century French reformer and a major theologian of the Protestant Reformation, who fled under duress from France to Switzerland. In Geneva, he continued to develop his ideas about salvation, with their emphasis on eternal damnation. He influenced a wide range of thinkers, including the Scottish preacher and reformer John Knox, a near contemporary, whose legacy is the Presbyterian Church, which in Scotland has been vastly influential.

I struggled with the idea of grace, which can be traced back easily to Augustine, who emphasized God's forgiveness, and the fact that enlightenment or salvation is not something we "earn" by doing good works. God simply poured on us his "saving grace," as Augustine writes in "On Nature and Grace."[5] He gives us a fresh life and with this grace "helps us as a medicine through the Mediator," who is Jesus. Augustine wanted to bring faith and works together. But the Reformation, especially in its Calvinist vein, stressed the absolute disconnect between faith and works, taking human merit out of the formula for salvation. Calvin says of Augustine on this subject: "For that matter, Augustine's view, or at any rate his manner of stating it, we must not entirely accept. For even though he admirably deprives man of all credit for righteousness and transfers it to God's grace, he still subsumes grace under sanctification, by which we are reborn in the newness of life, through the spirit."[6] Not surprisingly, perhaps, I found the Calvinism in Protestant thought too rigid, having been convinced that grace and works move happily together: one is inspired by the spirit to behave well, and to treat others as we would like ourselves to be treated. The idea of damnation, so prevalent in reformist theology, neither terrified nor inspired me. It just seemed like a bore.

During my seven years in Scotland as a young man, I sometimes attended chapel services that still showed the influence of this severe tradition, with its emphasis on damnation. I can't help but think of my old friend Alastair Reid, a poet (and son of a Calvinist minister) who once met a severe Presbyterian woman on a bright spring day: one of those rare days in Scotland when the sky is blue, the sun is blazing, and the grass is singing. Alastair said to her: "Such a lovely day, Miss Mackay." She replied, frowning: "Aye, but we'll pay for it." In a similar vein, I once said to my landlady before turning in for the night: "I'll see you tomorrow." She said, grimly: "If we're spared."

Nothing that encourages excessive regret or engenders fear of damnation is truly Christian. But I understand the need for repentance, which has its place in every practice, especially during Lent. It's a time for humbling ourselves, for a heightened awareness of our vulnerability, or weaknesses. In "Ash-Wednesday," one of his most bracing and beautiful poems, Eliot asked for a balanced approach to life: "Teach us to care and not to care." He quotes the Hail Mary here: "Pray for us sinners now and at the hour of our death." A full awareness of our own sinfulness, combined with an acute sense of our mortality, opens us to possibilities of the spirit. We're in effect preparing the ground for planting.

We live so briefly. I'm painfully aware of this, though I don't know how much time I have left. I fully understand that most of my life is behind me, and what is left is simply another of God's gifts, however long it lasts. But perhaps I could have said the same thing forty or even fifty years ago. It helps to keep the mutability of life in mind, the fact that suffering is part of who we are as creatures, and that nothing lasts. There is a sense of relief in this as well: we don't have to strive so much or covet the gifts or successes or good luck of others. We don't have to prove ourselves again and again. All we have to do is love God and love our neighbors as ourselves. These are the core commandments, the center of our faithfulness. And we are drawn

back to these essentials in Lent, when we're stripped of pretense, joining our fellow congregants to step forward to receive the ashes, this
sign of our emptiness, our vulnerability, or at least the vulnerability
of our flesh-in-time. We are, as Yeats writes in "Sailing to Byzantium,"
"fastened to a dying animal." That is our fate: bodies that came from
and return to dust.

The aura of Lent, with its penitential mood, envelops the church
during this season of preparation for Easter. The color purple predom-
inates: a sign of repentance. The confessional tone emerges, tinging
all prayers. The great praise term, *alleluia*, falls away. In my own prayer
life, I look for quiet during Lent, taking stock of my past, my present
transgressions: that word quite literally (*trans-gressus*) means "stepping
over the line," and it refers to places in my behavior where I fail to love
others as myself, where I fail to "seek God's face," that lovely phrase
from Psalm 27. I want to model the mercy of God, but that is hard: I
get angry with others at times. I can become woefully self-involved,
concerned about my "reputation" in the world, as if that mattered.
What fools we are, thinking we must push our way forward, when
there is no forward, no backward. During Lent, I often just sit in my
study, early in the morning, listening—or trying to listen—beyond
the monkey chatter in my head, leaning into the eternal silence, that
place of love, where we come into a sense of conjunction with God.

There is personal confession and public confession, and both are
necessary. We live in ourselves, and yet we live in the body of Christ,
as well as in the larger community. As Thoreau notes in *Walden*: "I
have three chairs in my house: one for solitude, two for friendship,
and three for society." We keep these chairs in mind as we move
through life. Public confession invites us to join with others, to become one body, with set goals and hopes, sharing an awareness of
the need for justice, even reparations. I was moved to read that the
German church, at the end of World War II, issued a public Confession of Guilt: "We accuse ourselves for not witnessing more cou-
rageously, for not praying more faithfully, for not believing more
joyously and for not loving more ardently. Now a new beginning is

to be made in our churches."[7] There is really never a time when this confession doesn't seem apt.

To make a new beginning matters, as we have lost our way, stepped off the path into error. Christians are perpetual beginners, always starting from scratch, aware of the human tendency to fall away from God, to become alienated from our best selves, to lose our commitment to justice, regeneration, and eventual resurrection. And all Christian thinking is, as I have suggested, Resurrection Thinking. It's about reconnecting—as in *re-ligio*—with the kingdom of God that lies within us. And Lenten meditations usher us into a place where that resurrection becomes, at least in theory, possible. It's all the work of preparation, which is why in church we often have Lenten study groups, where a small gathering looks at a certain text and reflects on the words, generating conversations as a community that help to bring us forward as a gathering or church. In private, as in public, we lean into beginnings, we pray and study, we grow into community through conversation and "gathering." This is the mood of Lent.

Holy Week is the last week of Lent. The drums roll, and the Easter Triduum looms—the long weekend that culminates in Easter Sunday. Our symbolic forty days in the desert—a period of self-reflection, repentance, and repositioning—come to an end. There are often services or ceremonies of one kind or another to mark this period, including Palm Sunday, a service that cheers the entry of Jesus on a donkey into Jerusalem, with elaborate rituals that often includes the distribution of palms. During the week, there is a ceremony called the Stations of the Cross, in which a small group moves around the church, in clockwise fashion, pausing briefly for prayers or meditations at the fourteen "stations," or positions, on the journey of Jesus from the Last Supper through the Resurrection. I love this odd, one-off ceremony. The stops reflect the agony of Jesus in the Garden (where he prayed before his arrest), his trials, his scourging (being beaten) and receiving the crown of thorns, his carrying the cross through the streets and falling under the weight of it, the help he gets from Simon of Cyrene, his being nailed to the cross itself, his words with the "thief" who repents of his sins, his death and burial, and, finally, his resurrection. These are familiar moments in what is called the Passion of Christ, and each of them is deliberately called into memory, reconsidered, absorbed.

One of the places on earth where this symbolic path has literal meaning is Jerusalem itself, along the Via Dolorosa, where for centuries pilgrims have walked along a route that begins at the Lion's Gate, at the Monastery of the Flagellation, and leads along a winding street to Church of the Holy Sepulcher, which now houses the Rock of Cavalry, where tradition holds that Jesus was crucified between two "thieves," the exact nature of their lawbreaking not being known. (At least since the early fourth century, this has been considered the actual site of the Crucifixion, though the evidence for this remains scant—as with so much about the ancient past.) I myself walked this route in 1989, and I often recall that experience, the passing under archways along narrow streets, with the scent of spices, from tiny stalls mingling with aromas of coffee, baking pitas, cat piss, and goat dung.

I think I'll never forget climbing this street toward the Church of the Holy Sepulcher with my father. He was, as noted earlier, a fundamentalist Christian; as such, he had a visceral sense of the literal aspects of the faith. I admired his concrete devotion to a reality that opened before him in Israel. He told me that this walk along the Via Dolorosa was, for him, the experience of a lifetime, and I was glad to be able to share this day beside him. I will never forget how, in the church itself, at the point where the cross is traditionally said to have been rooted, he crawled on his knees to the exact spot and kissed the ground. Afterward, his eyes blazed, tearfully, joyfully. In a way, he had come home.

In a sense, the conclusion of Holy Week, in real terms, brings us home, allows us to inhabit a place where we rest in God, in the promise of eternity that arrives with a full blast of trumpets on Easter Sunday. Over the three days of Easter, which is the Triduum, we move toward the moment of Resurrection, reliving this movement with an intensity not available during other parts of the Church Year.

▪ THE EASTER TRIDUUM

The Triduum is often called the Paschal Triduum—the word "paschal" refers to the Jewish Passover, or *pesach*, a celebration that recalls the flight of the Jews from their captivity in Egypt, when they had been subjected to humiliations and onerous labor. During the Passover, God struck at the homes of Egyptians, killing their firstborn, but he "passed over" the homes of those who had kept faith with him. It's a key part of the Jewish year, and it's the central weekend of the Christian calendar, with Easter as the culmination of the Church Year itself.

Easter properly begins with Maundy Thursday. That strange adjective refers to the Latin *mandatum*, or "commandment." Jesus gave a new commandment to his disciples: "Just as I have loved you, you must love one another" (John 13:34). The service associated with this commandment is one of sadness and fear as well as fellowship and recalls the Last Supper, when Jesus gathered his disciples in a room for a final meal before he was swept away and executed. Typically the congregation will come forward for the "foot washing," imitating Jesus, who washed the feet of his disciples. This was a stunning act, as described in John's Gospel, a servile one; it disturbs Peter, who says defiantly: "You shall never wash my feet" (John 13:9). But Jesus answers him in the next verse: "Unless I wash you, you have no part of me." There follows a remarkable statement by Jesus:

> Now that I, your Lord and Teacher, have washed your feet, you also should wash one another's feet. I have set you an example that you should do as I have done for you. Very truly I tell you, no servant is greater than his master, nor is a messenger greater than the one who sent him.

Jesus is "Lord and Teacher," but he is also the suffering servant. He washes our feet, as we wash the feet of others. "No servant is greater than his master," he said. That is, Jesus did not consider himself greater than God, as the son is not greater than the father. Jesus is the messenger of God, who sent him to give us this crucial (and challenging) teaching.

The theology of this statement is hugely controversial and complex as well. Is Jesus God? Yes and no. I think Harvey Cox puts this well in *The Future of Faith*, where he meditates on the difference between Jesus and Christ:

> "Christ" means more than Jesus. It also refers to the new skein of relationships that arose around him during and after his life. . . . Paul frequently speaks of the Christ who dwells within him and within the other followers. When, for example, he writes that among those who share the Spirit of Christ, "There is neither Jew nor Greek, there is neither slave nor free, there is neither male nor female, for all are one in Christ Jesus," he means something more extensive than the historical Jesus (Gal. 3:28). The Easter cycle, with all its harshness, joy, and impenetrability, tells of this enlargement of this historical Jesus story into the Christ story.[8]

Jesus has many faces, and in one of his roles he is certainly the servant of God, and the son of God; but each of us who follows him is equally a child of God, as he often tells us. God is within us. We follow him, joining one path to God. "I am the way," he says. That is, if you choose to follow the Way of Jesus, he is the way. His way is the way of servanthood, of loving one's neighbor as oneself, of doing good to those who harm you, of resting (and sometimes wrestling) with God in the silence of his creation, which is active and ongoing and is symbolized by the Resurrection. As the French priest and philosopher Pierre Teilhard de Chardin put it so well: "Creation, Incarnation and Redemption are seen to be no more than three complementary aspects of one and the same process."[9]

The Maundy Thursday service includes the washing of feet. This move mirrors the moment when Jesus bent to his knees and washed the probably dirty feet of his disciples, who were surprised by this, even loath to have him do it. For me, this is a shocking thing to do. I don't like to touch the foot of someone else in this way, nor do I like having my own feet washed. But the gesture brings me, with the congregation, into intimate contact.

This service ends with the dramatic "stripping of the altar," when everything is put away, and the altar lies bare. It's a blunt and rude process, with candelabras put aside, the cross removed, all vessels and fine linens packed up. The cold stone of the altar lies bare, representing the body of Jesus, the nude corpse of the suffering Christ, who is stripped for torture. Everything is lost so that, in the course of the Triduum, everything can be rediscovered and renewed. The congregation files out of the church in silence, and darkness follows.

Good Friday arrives the next day, the phrase itself being a corruption of "God's Friday," although "good" is also suggestive, as a term of holiness. This is the day of the Crucifixion, and it's distressing to anyone who can imagine a crucifixion, surely one of the most horrifying forms of capital punishment, a totalizing instance of suffering. Services on this day will include readings from the Gospels, especially those connected with the Crucifixion, often centered on the seven last sentences of Jesus as he died:

> Father, forgive them, for they know not what they do.
> Today you will be with me in paradise.
> Behold your son: behold your mother.
> My God, my God, why has thou forsaken me?
> I thirst.
> It is finished.
> Father, into your hands I commend my spirit.

Each of these carries weight, and the words live in history. (It's worth noting that the famous fourth statement is a direct quote from

Psalm 22, again suggesting that the Gospel writers took great pains to connect the story of Jesus with the Hebrew scriptures.) Prayers follow the readings, during which time the congregation is asked to remember those in need, those who suffer as Christ has suffered. Sometimes there is a ritual called the Veneration of the Cross, although this can also be part of the Maundy Thursday service: a bare cross is brought to the front of the church, and the congregation—one by one—comes forward to kneel before it, even to kiss it. The ritual dates to the early fourth century, when Saint Helen came upon what she believed was a fragment of the cross in Jerusalem.

Needless to say, the cross is the ultimate icon, a symbol of sacrifice, with its undeniable power to transfix, and it has been for centuries a primary symbol of the faith. We must all die, of course; Jesus, in effect, perfects the art of dying here, releasing himself at last into the hands of eternity in a mood of forgiveness. The horizontal limbs of the cross represent the outstretched arms of Jesus, a posture of opening, a generosity that everybody who follows the Way should try to emulate. There is nothing one holds to oneself. One should give and give more. The vertical axis reaches to the sky above, to "heaven," and it digs into the earth as well, grounded. So much has been written about the meaning of the cross, but I come back to the moving words of Oscar Romero, who spoke out against poverty, social injustice, and mass killings in El Salvador, where he served as bishop until, in 1980, he was assassinated while offering mass in a hospital chapel. He said: "We have never preached violence, except the violence of love, which left Christ nailed to a cross, the violence that we must each do to ourselves to overcome our selfishness and such cruel inequalities among us. The violence we preach is not the violence of the sword, the violence of hatred. It is the violence of love, of brotherhood, the violence that wills to beat weapons into sickles for work."[10]

Protestant traditions exclude communion at Good Friday services, using bread and wine that was consecrated before Maundy Thursday. In my childhood, as a Baptist, these were deemed ecumenical services, meaning that Christian churches from various traditions (usually Protestant) came together to join forces. This tradition is widespread, and it's heartening to see—however briefly—a healing of the body of Christ, as the many parts merge in recognition of the importance of Good Friday, which somehow "resists being talked about, even thought about, for long,"[11] as Auden once said. (Despite making this authoritative statement, Auden wrote a brilliant poem about Good Friday in his book *Nones*, and there are some stirring poems on the subject by many poets, from George Herbert's "The Sacrifice" to Geoffrey Hill's "Canticle for Good Friday.")

Holy Saturday is an in-between time, a day between death and resurrection. Christians look backward to the agony of the execution, the bleeding body rags of Jesus, the sad burial in the tomb, when even his closest disciples considered everything lost. But Christians also look forward to Easter Sunday. This anxious, transitional space between two worlds is one we know all too well, being human. Holy Saturday unfolds in this uncertain space, as we recall the tomb where Jesus lies, his soul on a perilous journey as he dives into depths in the so-called Harrowing of Hell—a legend without scriptural basis that suggests Jesus plunged to hell itself, into the underworld. World myth often recalls the descent of a hero to a dark hole, a place of mental or physical confinement, as when Jonah was swallowed by a whale and passed three days in the belly of the whale or when Gilgamesh (in the Sumerian epic from 2100 BCE) descended into hell on a search for immortal life. Examples abound in all religious traditions.

It's a descent we can all imagine, and this is a good time in the cycle of the Church Year for such a plunge. It's a shocking day when we may begin the work of owning our own death, accepting it, even swallowing it. Owning one's own death means having imaginative possession of it. It means being aware that the human body is not remotely permanent, and it should not be. Can you imagine a permanent tree? The *psyche*, or soul, remains a work in progress, with creation (and resurrection) always active, at least as a possibility. Breaking through the barrier of death means breaking the body, opening it up, allowing the soul to reform, reformulate its meaning and context. In losing our life, we find ourselves: "In my end is my beginning," as Eliot wrote in "East Coker." But we must fully empty ourselves of our physical presence in time; the glass has to be drained of this fluid, life; but it begins to refill almost immediately, just as after night the dawn gradually wakens, and slowly the light refills the day. All of nature moves in these cycles: day and night, the seasons. There is no reason not to see ourselves as part of this continuous cycle.

Holy Saturday is also known as the Sacred Sabbath (Latin: *Sabbatum Sanctum*). It symbolizes a profound and frantic emptiness in which each of us experiences (symbolically) the absence of life, yet with an awareness of the life to come. This liminal space is truly one of the great gifts of the Triduum: a timeless day that Jesus has entered for us, has experienced fully by diving into depths of nonbeing. And we, as living and dying creatures, experience a transitional anxiety as well, aware that on the other side of the river there may be hope, even while nearly sinking back into the darkness. This is a space we inhabit every day at some point, shifting from foot to foot, from fear to hope: the human condition encapsulated.

The evening of Holy Saturday, a vigil begins when the congregation gathers outside the church in darkness. We carry candles into the dark church, and "The light of Christ" may be chanted. Readings from various texts proclaim the coming brightness, the vanquishing of dark. This is frequently a very long service, with a summoning of scriptural passages that recall a variety of sacrifices depicted in the Hebrew scriptures, as in the sacrifice of Isaac in Genesis 22:1–18. My favorite among many Easter Vigil readings is Ezekiel 37:1–14, where we hear about the Valley of Dry Bones, with a plaintive question hovering in the textual air: "Can these bones live?" God answers: "Behold, I will cause breath to enter into you, and ye shall live." The service ends with a shout: *Christ is risen!* And a response: *He is risen indeed!*

The phrase resonates through the night into morning. I will never forget joining an Easter procession through the streets of Amalfi, in southern Italy, with the crowd chanting: *Cristo è risorto!* The thrill of that phrase never fails to excite me. It's a way of saying: I'm alive, I'm risen, I will live forever!

So Easter arrives at last, the vital day, a pivotal scene in the story of Jesus. (The word "Easter" may derive from Eostre, the Anglo-Saxon goddess of fertility and spring.) What remains astonishing is that we never see Jesus actually wake up from the dead, not in any of the Gospels. The event happens offstage, in the wings of the theater of the mind. The account of what happened on Easter morning varies in each Gospel, but John seems most compelled by this event, and the tale is drawn out fully by its author, who describes what happens when Mary Magdalene—perhaps the best friend of Jesus—arrives at the tomb and wonders why the stone has been rolled away. The empty tomb puzzles and frightens her.

When Jesus speaks to her, she assumes he's a gardener. Not until he says her name does she recognize her friend. She says, in their native Aramaic, *Rabboni!* This means teacher, and the vernacular marks its authenticity, for her. As it happens, Mary Magdalene is not the only one who doesn't recognize Jesus. Several accounts of Christ appearing to disciples after the Resurrection emphasize his inscrutability. He is not the man they knew. This truth dominates the story of two men on the Road to Emmaus. Jesus appears beside them as they walk out of Jerusalem, and he listens as they talk about the Crucifixion, which they have left behind them. He feigns ignorance of this event, and they express shock. How could he not know about the death of Jesus, the great teacher? He plays along, letting them think he's someone else. Not until he begins to say thanks over the meal that evening do the scales fall from their eyes. It's Jesus! But what happens? *Poof.* He disappears. The vision of the Resurrected Jesus can't be sustained. It's beyond human comprehension. It's too bright, even blinding, and beyond understanding in normal terms.

Even those closest to Jesus fail to recognize him in his resurrected form, so what hope do we have, two thousand years later? There seems little chance of knowing him again, and these Gospel stories gesture toward a larger truth, that the Resurrection is not the Great Resuscitation, not a mere blowing of life into a dead body, as we saw with the story of Lazarus. This is different. It's the mystery of Easter, which is the most precious mystery that will be found in Christianity. Jesus rose from the dead, as we shall one day, transmogrified, magically transformed, changed into what Christians call the "glorified body," which is not in time, not easily understood by our frail minds. This resurrection signifies fulfillment, an entering into enlightenment in such a way that we cannot be removed from this special place that is no place, a time beyond time itself.

Easter delivers the message of God's love in operation in the world, and it's a fertile one. Yes, "the dead will rise, imperishable, and we shall be transformed," says Paul in 1 Corinthians 15:52. But that implies a larger truth, that we join together in community. It's the Kingdom of God being realized, much as in the spring the dry seeds of autumn, which lay dormant through winter, startle into life. Whitman, a poet of resurrection, imagined this composting of dead bodies, which he likens to the grass that suddenly rises through the soil:

> Yet Behold!
> The grass covers the prairies,
> The bean bursts noiselessly through the mould in the garden,
> The delicate spear of the onion pierces upward,
> The apple-buds cluster together on the apple-branches,
> The resurrection of the wheat appears
>   with pale visage out of its graves.

This is resurrection, which permeates our poetry and song. "Rise heart; thy Lord is risen," writes George Herbert in "Easter," in which he imagines us taking Jesus by the hand and soaring with him from the grave. In a similar vein, Thomas Merton, in his *Seasons of Celebration*, says, "Let us declare His power, by living as free men who have been called by Him out of darkness into his admirable light." In the church of my youth, we sang, "Up from the grave he arose / With a mighty triumph o'er his foes." Now I tend to prefer Handel or Bach, who found Easter a fitting subject: my own favorite here is the *Easter Oratorio* of Bach, less known than his *Saint Matthew Passion* but shattering in its beauty and poise. Of course Handel's *Messiah* also accompanies Easter nicely, especially the Hallelujah Chorus, one of the best-loved pieces of music in the West, with its triumphant refrain: "And He shall reign forever and ever."

The Fifty Days

The celebration of the Easter Triduum dates to the earliest days of Christianity, as the first followers of Jesus must have felt a strong need to return to the scene of their profound Good Friday trauma and recovery. After Easter, Christians in their worship resumed the saying of alleluias, that sign of thanksgiving. Fasts were, of course, suspended. The joyous feeling of Easter uplift extended for the seven weeks that followed, a period in which the joy of the Resurrection continued. Indeed, the week after Easter is often called Bright Week (or Easter Week or Pascha Week) and continues until the following Sunday, often known as Thomas Sunday, as that liturgy is sometimes focused on "Doubting Thomas," the disciple who needed literal proof of the Resurrection.

By the second century CE a fresh tradition had arisen: the fifty days after Easter that lead up to the Pentecost (meaning "fiftieth" in Greek), when God poured out the Holy Spirit on his people. There were, in fact, forty days from the Resurrection to the Ascension, as described by Luke in the first chapter of Acts. The Ascension is described importantly (though very briefly) in Luke 24:50–53: "When he had led them out to the vicinity of Bethany, he lifted up his hands and blessed them. While he was blessing them, he left them and was

taken up into heaven. Then they worshiped him and returned to Jerusalem with great joy." The concision of this exhilarating scene hasn't
deterred endless gifted painters from imagining it, often with luxuri-
ous detail. I admire the versions by Giotto and Mantegna, Rembrandt
and Benjamin West, to name only the obvious examples. Countless
shimmering icons in the Eastern Orthodox tradition focus on this
event. The return of Jesus to his father obviously excites the imagination, and it's one of the happy mysteries to contemplate: an image
one can re-create in one's mind with ease, a picture of Jesus lifting his
arms to the heaven, floating skyward, absorbed at last.

Yet the Easter season properly concludes ten days later, with Pentecostal fire marking the beginning of Ordinary Time.

▪ ORDINARY TIME

I love Ordinary Time, the six months of "downtime" that follows the
Easter season. But let's focus on the Pentecost first, the event that
opens this period, a startling mythic occasion in its own right. The
remaining disciples (minus Judas, the betrayer of Jesus) met in Jerusalem ten days after the Ascension for Shavuoth, the Festival of
Weeks—essentially a harvest festival absorbed into Jewish ritual at
some point in history and commemorating the giving of the Law (it
was celebrated fifty days after the second day of Passover). The Christian feast of Pentecost mimics Jewish tradition here, though it has its
own specific meanings and bright imagery, signifying the gift of the
Holy Spirit to humanity.

Mary, the mother of Jesus, gathered with other followers of the
Way in a room in Jerusalem. The story unfolds with drama in Acts
2:1–6:

> When the day of Pentecost had arrived, they were all
> together in one place. And suddenly came a sound from
> heaven like that of a rushing wind, and it filled the house

where they sat. And there appeared to them forked tongues like fire, and it hovered upon each of them. And they were all filled with the Holy Ghost, and began to speak with other tongues, as the Spirit allowed. Now Jews and other devout men lived in Jerusalem, out of every nation under heaven. Now when this was relayed abroad, the group met together, astounded because every man heard them speak in his own language.

God had a gift for the followers of Jesus: the Holy Spirit—the third (and least understood) part of the Trinity, which brings with it a spirit of wildness, as in the gabble of tongues described above. This is a time, as Peter said, when the sun turns black, and when the moon "turns to blood" (Acts 2:20). One sees the Pentecostal fire in certain small sects of Christianity, where this wildness catches fire in a spirit, and an individual speaks in an unintelligible language: "glossolalia" is the term for this "speaking in tongues."

It's worth pausing to consider the fulfillment here: the emergence of the Triune God, the Trinity. Saint Augustine writes, "There is no subject where error is more dangerous, research more laborious, and discovery more fruitful than the oneness of the Trinity."[12] This difficult concept, quite naturally, puzzled theologians for centuries, and it still does. God is traditionally pictured as a father, a kind of Zeus figure, the creator spirit; he is high above us, abstract, unapproachable, even terrifying: the word "wrath" occurs in conjunction with Jehovah hundreds of times in the Hebrew scriptures. This is the God we often meet in biblical stories, where his vengeful nature can trouble the faithful. By contrast, Jesus—as the human face of God—remains approachable, comforting. He walks beside us, one of us. But then—after the Ascension—he was gone, although his followers continued (as they do now) to feel his presence as "the son of God," someone who directs us toward the *Christos*, the mystical savior. Which brings us to the Holy Spirit.

Is this spirit even a "who," or should we perhaps call it "it" or something else? I like to think of the Holy Spirit as the God within us, welling up, soothing in the night and calling us to commitment during the day. It's an aid and an abettor, helping those who need assistance in the hard work of sustaining trust in God. We read in John about this mystical "wind" (note that the Latin word for wind is *spiritus*): "The wind blows where it pleases, and you can't tell where it comes from or where it's going. So it is with everyone born of the spirit" (John 3:8). There is a certain capriciousness here in the notion of the spirit that may unsettle at first; but it's like inspiration itself, which often comes from nowhere, and which holds us, sustains us, through life.

The idea of a divine spirit precedes Christianity. Think back to the passage from Numbers in which God helps Moses by giving him and "the elders of the people" the assistance of the spirit. "And the Lord came down in a cloud, and spoke unto him, and took of the spirit that was upon him," we are told, "and it came to pass, that, when the spirit rested upon them, they prophesied, and did not cease" (Numbers 11:24–25). The Holy Spirit was used to establish a covenant between God and Israel; in like manner, the Pentecost marked a new covenant between God and the people of God, who found (and continue to find) fresh access to him through the operations of the spirit. (It's interesting that the arrival of the Holy Spirit becomes for Christians what the giving of the Law was for the Jews.)

At the Pentecostal feast, Peter—who increasingly (with James, the brother of Jesus) became the leader of the Way of Jesus in Jerusalem—offered a sermon (Acts 2:14–36) in which he laid out the basic tenets of the faith, regarding the Pentecost as a fulfillment with parallels to events described in the Hebrew scriptures, as in Joel 2:28: "And it shall come to pass afterward, that I will pour out my spirit upon all flesh; and your sons and your daughters shall prophesy, and your old men shall dream dreams, your men shall see visions." This is lovely. As it were, Eliot could never get the Pentecost out of his head, and he uses the images of the tongues of flame at the very end of his *Four Quartets*:

> And all shall be well and
> All manner of thing shall be well
> When the tongues of flames are in-folded
> Into the crowned knot of fire
> And the fire and the rose are one.

The unity that Eliot suggests here, with the fire and the rose united, a symbol of union with God, allows all who follow the Way of Jesus to move forward into our lives, into Ordinary Time.

So what happens in Ordinary Time? We follow Jesus by ministering to the sick, the neglected, prisoners, those who require our attention and service. I often think of this as the ministry of presence. We serve by simply offering ourselves, by waiting on the sick or shaken, by calling a friend in difficult straits, by waiting with someone at the doctor's office, by sitting at the foot of a bed in a hospital or nursing home. We become missionaries by helping where we can to feed the hungry or promote peace in whatever small ways we can, although these may seem trivial at first glance. But nothing is trivial, and it's not worth thinking about the final products of our activities, as we can't weigh them, and they will never be measured by weight or volume.

During Ordinary Time, we work on our own spiritual lives, praying and meditating, reading the scriptures, reading books and poems, or whatever material furthers our thoughts along healthful lines. We attend services, worshipping God, drawing inspiration from the example of others. We go about our business, trying to stay in touch with God as we proceed. It's not possible to "pray without ceasing," as Paul suggested; but it's perfectly reasonable to attempt to bring our minds into focus, to find the God within us, as we can. There are, of course, so many things that require our attention as we attempt to follow the Way of Jesus. These involve, as I suggest in the final chapter of this book, five things: prayer, observance, discipline, thought, and action.

This is the second phase of Ordinary Time, the first phase being right after Christmas (after the Epiphany) and before Lent, and it has only one high point, which is the Feast of the Transfiguration, on August 6. This celebration recalls the time when Jesus took Peter, James, and John to a mountaintop in Galilee. As they watched in awe, their teacher was lifted into the sky and transformed, or "transfigured." Matthew and Luke follow the lead of Mark in describing this event, regarding it as something special. Matthew expands on the narrative with details not found in the other Gospels: "And he was transfigured before them, and his face shone like the sun, and his garments turned white as the light itself." It's not surprising that painters have found this an appealing, even irresistible, subject: Jesus in the sky, with two Hebrew prophets (Moses and Elijah) on either side of him. His garments shimmer, otherworldly, as God speaks: "This is my beloved son, in whom I am well pleased. Listen to him" (Matthew 17:5).

The transformation of the "normal" body of Jesus into a heavenly one, a "glorified" body, prefigures the Resurrection itself. Aquinas suggests that the Transfiguration is quite useful, coming where it does just before the end of Jesus's life, as a way of showing his most devout followers what the goal might be: the resurrected body. It's a miracle, a sign of the life to come, its full potential. As Norman O. Brown says: "Christ is able to project the life-giving power of his glorified body without spatial limitation."[13]

This miracle lifts us up in the midst of Ordinary Time, but one has to settle back into the rhythms of this phase of the Church Year, accepting the gift of each day and releasing it at night, sensing the growth to harvest, the arrival of early fall, with its intimations of mortality. In some ways, this is my favorite time of year, with the corn at its full height in the fields, glistening in the sunlight. Indeed, the liturgical color that dominates in Ordinary Time is green, meant to suggest growth. I'm reminded of one of my favorite passages in poetry, some lines from Stevens's "Esthétique du Mal," where he imagines the "non-physical people" in heaven, those already in their glorified state, looking down at the rows of corn in the summer fields; when they see the "green corn gleaming," they experience the "minor of what we feel." This experience, in Ordinary Time, is for Stevens "[T]he reverberating psalm, the right chorale."

Looking at the Church Year broadly, one sees that the first six months, from Advent through Pentecost, focus on the life of Christ, marking the key events, giving these events their full liturgical weight, seeing them as markers in the evolving life of the individual who follows the Way of Jesus. We move, with him, from birth to resurrection, transformed by the gift of the Holy Spirit at Pentecost. This ushers us into the second half of the year, the major phase of Ordinary Time, which to some extent is about the life of the church, the living members of the body of Christ, who reach into the world and transform it, culminating on the last day before advent begins, with Christ the King Sunday, when (this is a fairly recent liturgical feast) the church commits itself to justice. One common reading of this feast day is from the affecting words of Jesus on service to others in Mark 10:42–45:

> You have seen that those recognized as rulers over the Gentiles lord it over them, and their superiors make their authority over them felt. But it must never be so among you, my followers. Those among you who wish to become great will be servants; whoever wishes to be first among you will be the slave of everyone. Just as the Son of Man did not come to be served but himself to serve.

It's a pity that so many Christians have let the Church Year slip away from them. If anything, they associate the idea with Christmas and Easter, but without a full sense of the cycle that culminates at these two key points in the calendar. The liturgical round is based on the agricultural round, with planting in the spring, the slow growth of summer, with fall harvest, the dip into winter's freeze after the stripping away of life from the plant world, then the gradual return of spring, the gurgle of underground streams, melting snow, warmer days, and the need for planting again. Even those of us who live far from this pattern understand it. It survives in our bones, part of our ancestral inheritance, and we carry the archetypes of planting and harvesting in our souls. The Church Year, which follows the life of Christ, runs in these seasonal grooves, which are ancient and—quite literally—God-given.

I suppose I'm lucky to live in the deep country, where it's impossible to forget the agricultural round, as I smell the fertilizer in the spring, I see the corn growing, and I watch the work of mowing in late summer and fall. I live in a part of the world where the seasons move distinctly, with bold colors and a complete change of clothes. The temperature shifts dramatically, as does the landscape. In a nearby woods, I usually hike several times a week in each season, even in heavy snows. And it's there, in the church of the woods, that I discover my own absence and find, now and then, the presence of God: that silence at the heart of things. It's there and then that I find myself able to comprehend a bit more fully than in the rest of my life what Stevens in "Sunday Morning" called "the old dependency of day and night," that beautiful complementarity. In full appreciation of the turning seasons, moving within the rhythms of the Church Year, it seems possible to find rebirth, and consider myself part of the kingdom of God that Jesus said was there, within us.

FOUR

HOW TO BE A CHRISTIAN

The essential thing is for us to hear God's word and discover from it
how to respond to him.

—*Balthasar*

When one has once fully entered the realm of love, the world—no
matter how imperfect—becomes rich and beautiful, it consists solely
of opportunities for love.

—*Kierkegaard*, Works of Love

As I've done throughout this book, I often go back to Eliot, whose
work—especially the later work—offers a great deal to those seeking
language about transcendental realities. I once had a conversation
about him with I. A. Richards, a literary critic who was a good friend
of Eliot's in the early twenties. He recalled Eliot coming to stay with
him for a weekend in Cambridge, where Richards was teaching. As
was his custom, Richards brought his guest a cup of tea in his bedroom on Sunday morning; but it surprised him that Eliot had slipped
out of the house without a word. At midday, Eliot returned, and he
sheepishly admitted to the atheistic Richards that he had gone to
mass at the local Anglican church. Richards was surprised, and he
questioned Eliot, who said he found it worth going, although he had

not committed to the faith. He told Richards that he had begun a journey, and he had no idea where it would lead.

Eliot would commit to a specific path, Anglo-Catholic Christianity, and remain devoted to this practice, its forms and truths, until his death in 1965, and his writings in poetry and prose would reflect this choice. Yet this faith choice was a complex affair, mingling aspects of Eastern religion, especially Hinduism and Buddhism, which he had studied at Harvard, with an awareness of variant Christian traditions of spirituality. He grew up in a mainstream American Protestant church, but I suspect that Boston Unitarianism (the faith of his family) probably struck him as thin gruel, with rectitude having to stand in for genuine spiritual growth.

Eliot's work in the thirties—I'm thinking of "Ash-Wednesday" and his play *Murder in the Cathedral*—bear witness to his new commitment to the Christian faith in its Anglican modalities. Note that I don't use the word "conversion" here, as Eliot would not have liked that. The notion of a conversion of the Pauline variety would have seemed to him—as a rather straightlaced American from St. Louis with roots in puritanical New England—too emotional, flamboyant, even false. No Road to Damascus for him. Rather, he pursued a quiet path that required discipline, a careful tilling of the fields. Intellect and emotion, for him, fused as he explored the gradually realizing kingdom of God. And there is probably no better record of this than the *Four Quartets*, which unfolded over a period of several years, beginning with "Burnt Norton," in 1935. Eliot quickly saw that the first quartet (each one a five-part sequence that meditates on a particular place and theme) offered a frame on which he could weave a series of quartets, and he did, with "East Coker" begun in 1937 and published in 1940. "The Dry Salvages," the third quartet, seems to have come rapidly, and he published it in February 1941, a very bleak time in British history, with London under siege from Nazi bombs. One feels that pressure in this quartet, with its evocation of "the voices wailing" and the "withering of withered flowers." He invites his readers to "[r]epeat a prayer . . . on behalf of women who have seen their sons or husbands / Setting forth, and not returning."

In such desperate times, he sees that those around him eagerly looked for ways to control time, to anticipate the future, perhaps in the hope of comfort, if not reassurance. And so people threw themselves into various popular practices or techniques—trying to foretell a future that can't be foretold in the hopes of getting control over time. They dropped tea leaves in the sink, looking for patterns. They drew lots, or tried to read palms or choose cards from a pack at random, looking for signs and omens. They turned to drugs or psychotherapy. In the latter, they explored "the womb or tomb or dreams." In every instance, they attempted to see a pattern that might explain to them the meaning of their lives, its purpose or direction. This activity, Eliot suggests, grew frenzied in a period of war, a time of "distress of nations." The search for meaning became quite pointless, Eliot seems to argue, having its roots in the secular dimension, the thin topsoil of contemporary life.

At this point in "The Dry Salvages" come what for me are the most formidable, eloquent, and genuinely useful lines in the poem, and ones that I will use as a kind of template for studying the practice of Christianity.

> But to apprehend
> The point of intersection of the timeless
> With time, is an occupation for the saint—
> No occupation either, but something given
> And taken, in a lifetime's death in love,
> Ardour and selflessness and self-surrender.
> For most of us, there is only the unattended
> Moment, the moment in and out of time,
> The distraction fit, lost in a shaft of sunlight,
> The wild thyme unseen, or the winter lightning

Or the waterfall, or music heard so deeply
That it is not heard at all, but you are the music
While the music lasts. These are only hints and guesses,
Hints followed by guesses; and the rest
Is prayer, observance, discipline, thought and action.
The hint half guessed, the gift half understood, is Incarnation.

These lines, for me, lay the groundwork for Christian living. They offer a pattern that is immensely productive, and I will move through the five key points—prayer, observance, discipline, thought, and action—with an eye toward establishing these as cornerstones of Christian practice.

Eliot allows that there are "saints" among us who spend "a lifetime's death in love" trying to discern the "point of intersection of the timeless / With time." What does that mean? In orthodox Catholic versions of Christianity, saints are quite literal—recently we saw Mother Teresa elevated to sainthood, for instance. She took her place among roughly ten thousand saints. The idea is that one can actually pray to these figures with the expectation that they will speak to God in heaven on our behalf, making an intercession. There are, I'm sure, countless examples of "miracles" that have occurred over many centuries, and those at the receiving end of these have attested to the powers of this or that particular saint.

I don't think it's profitable to dwell on the reality of these accounts. Suffice it to say that many Christians over the centuries have found it healing to turn to a particular saint. These are often, more or less, the equivalents of local spirits, or they have some particular appeal for the person in need. I myself often appeal to the Virgin Mary when I pray the rosary, which I do regularly. For me, Mary is the archetype of motherhood, the feminine side of God. I like that about her, and it doesn't matter to me whether the actual Mary in heaven is listening. That seems beside the point. Her presence is, for me, generous and comforting, appealing on many levels. I find myself able to connect to God through her presence in my prayers. She creates an opening that I can feel. For me, that is sufficient reason to invoke her name in prayers.

But, as Eliot says, few of us have any hope for sainthood (or would set off on a path that would lead there, such as joining a monastery). That is the work of a lifetime, but we all seek an awareness of the transcendent, an experience of the "moment in and out of time," the apprehension of time's solubility. Eliot had learned from one of his early teachers, Henri Bergson (with whom he studied in Paris) about time as *durée*. This notion came from Bergson's doctoral thesis, in which he drew a distinction between the real experience of time in ordinary life—he called this "real duration" (*durée réelle*)—and the rigidly spatial clock time that we overlay in an attempt to graph time in a linear way. He thought of the latter as a misguided attempt to impose spatial concepts on what was in reality an experience beyond space itself, unbounded by anything classical physics could measure. Time itself, as Bergson said, comes to us in the form of discrete moments or limited perceptions, flashes of reality. The measurement of time is an illusion: "We give a mechanical explanation of a fact and then substitute the explanation for the fact itself," Bergson wrote.

Eliot combines the Bergsonian idea with the well-known Hindu idea of time as nonlinear reality. In Hinduism, as in Christianity, God is timeless: a kind of enduring and pure consciousness at the center of the universe. God is "the still point of the turning wheel." He is here, now, always. Time as clock time or daily time, what one might trace on the face of a clock or calendar, is simply a manifestation of God that collapses into the black hole of the Absolute.

So we have (at least) two ways of thinking about time, but it's difficult fully to comprehend them, or to integrate them. As Eliot suggests, they are interdependent: one needs clock time to get to eternal time, to conquer it.

We have all experienced these glimmers of Reality (I use the capital letter to lift the word above everyday reality). Those intimations come to us at unattended moments, often when we're least prepared to make use of them. They can be so fleeting we can't believe in their significance, almost can't believe they happened. These spots of time are strung together over a lifetime like occasional pearls on a very long strand. And it's only rare people who manage to focus on these, to break through linear time in any sustained way: Eliot's "saints," who through decades of prayer and contemplation manage to access God or them.

Eliot understood that most of us, himself included, lack the persistence of the saint or the mystic's wild thirst for the Absolute. Instead there is "only the unattended / Moment, the moment in and out of time." And there is also "The distraction fit, lost in a shaft of sunlight" or, perhaps when walking in the woods, "The wild thyme unseen," which suggests a presence felt but not fully experienced. But there is also the "music heard so deeply / That it is not heard at all, but you are the music / While the music lasts." These are periods of total absorption, when eternal time seizes us, half by chance, and takes us for a little dance. I suspect most of us know what Eliot's talking about here.

These moments are called "hints and guesses," and that's about as far as Eliot will go. He's not a fundamentalist, willing to offer certainty, willing to say here is God: the absolute served on a platter. Fundamentalism, with its iron certainties, held no appeal for him. (It's worth recalling that the term "fundamentalist" goes back only to 1920, when a Baptist layman came up with the term, alluding to a series of literal-minded pamphlets called "The Fundamentals" that had been published a few years before. While a literalist view of Christianity reaches back many centuries, this was never a consciously defined movement, nor a sustained theological viewpoint. Medieval theologians, for instance, understood fully well that there are various levels of reading the truth, and that mythic readings or understandings occupied the highest of these levels.[1]) Eliot was content to follow inklings, intimations of immortality, surmises, accepting whatever the sensual world offered and the mind could summon in response. He turned his eyes upward in prayerful expectation.

Within Christian practice, in fact, everything begins and ends with prayer. So we will turn to that first.

▪ PRAYER

Two things appear true: most of us pray, and yet the word means very different things to different people. In a recent survey, the Pew Research Center found that 55 percent of Americans prayed every day.[2] Interestingly, in a 2013 British poll reported in the *Guardian*, only one in seven respondents claimed they would "never" pray.[3] The most arresting fact to emerge from this survey was that it was the youngest group, those in their twenties, who had the least objection to praying. All of this surveying, of course, begs a few larger questions: What does it mean to pray? Is it enough to close one's eyes and think for a minute? Does one have to address God or enter prayer with some expectation of concrete results?

I find the work of Hans Urs von Balthasar useful in thinking about prayer. In *Prayer* (1986), his seminal work, he examines the nature and practice of prayer. He separates Christian prayer from the objectless meditation of some Eastern practices, in which one does not have any "goal" or point of focus, and suggests that Christian prayer involves a direct and intentional participation in the Absolute. It's a way of connecting to the timelessness of God. And it may involve a gaze at the Trinity itself, the triune flame, or at the Incarnate Word—the divine *logos*. Balthasar argues that we are creatures with a mystery in our hearts; we each live with a secret garden inside that is neglected and forgotten, and prayer offers a key to open the gates of that magical place, allowing us to unlock something already there, if unexplored.

It is through Christ—the Incarnation of the Word—that prayer becomes possible. When Jesus said, "I am the way," he referred to himself as the bridge between human beings and God, between the time-bound and the timeless. Needless to say, we often see Jesus praying in the Gospels, as it's almost always the first thing he does before a hard or problematic choice. For instance, we see him withdraw to pray in the Garden of Gethsemane in a time of massive stress, turbulence, and dislocation—the eve of the Crucifixion. Prayer becomes the bridge to stability for him, as for us; it opens a path to the center, which is God's "all in all."

In Balthasar's philosophy of prayer, each member of the Trinity comes into play in the course of this activity: "There is the Father who predestines and chooses us and adopts us as his children; the Son who interprets the Father to us and gives him to us in his self-surrender unto death and the mystery of the bread; there is the Spirit who implants God's life in our souls and makes it known."[4] One way to think of this is that we emanate from God, are continuous with him, though separate as we grow into our distinct selves. And yet we are "chosen in Christ before the foundation of the world," as one reads in Ephesians 1:14. So in a sense we're already in conversation with God, and God speaks through us when we pray. The words that form in our heads are the words that assemble to create us, in God's mind: a kind of weird but suggestive reversal of the usual expectations.

It was for me a revelation to understand that one way of praying was simply to let words come, and to assume these words appear in some relation to God, as we emanate from God. So God is speaking to us in our own vernacular. And then, of course, there is holy silence: listening for the white noise of creation, which happens all the time, without ceasing, and is timeless as well as infinitely generative. This is, again, something that we experience as "before" us, although I dislike the chronological use of time here. It's "after" us as well. Mostly it is "during" us, the ongoing white-hot point of creation where we experience divinity itself, and where change is everything, the continuous transformations that we call "life."

The possibilities of prayer, what Stevens calls "the bread of faithful speech," are endless. One can frame the practice in many dimensions, and there is such a long and varied history of contemplation and prayer that I can simply gesture here in that direction to suggest that the cornerstone of religious practice is prayer. Talking to God is a way of participating in the living spirit of God. It's a way of finding God within ourselves, the "paradise within" that Milton wrote about in *Paradise Lost*. I don't think one can get far in any faith practice without some form of quiet contemplation of the Godhead, listening for God, allowing the spirit to inform us, lift us, teach us. And I would suggest that prayer is more a form of listening than anything else—miles from the prayerlike petitions that arise naturally in the course of the day, as in: "Oh God, my car is making funny noises. Please let it not break down until I get to the football game."

Balthasar suggests that prayer "is a conversation in which God's word has the initiative and we, for the moment, can be nothing more than listeners. The essential thing is for us to hear God's word and discover from it how to respond to him."[5] But of course we often can't separate "God's word" from our own words, which are the stuff of God, our love responding to his love, his love becoming manifest in our own phrasing, our feelings, our effort to incline our hearts in his direction. We experience the Trinity in prayer, too, as Balthasar and many other theologians have noted.

An easy way to think about the Trinity comes from Richard Rohr, a Franciscan theologian, who has often said that God is the divine experience "above" or "outside" us, the distant but undeniable force of creation. Jesus as "the son" is somehow "beside us." As the human face of God, he moves between two realms, at once thoroughly conversant with our everyday needs and the austerity of God. He is "the way" in that he models for us how to move between here and there, between clock time and eternal time. He is our friend. He is ourselves, as we take on the mind of Christ as he does: Christ here being *christos*, the messiah, who entered Jesus of Nazareth and became him, fully human but divine as well. The Holy Spirit, the third and least understood member of the Trinity, is God within us, moving from our deepest center, infinitely there. As Balthasar writes: "The Holy Spirit is always there from the revelation of the Word." That is, knowledge of the Word doesn't come only from human intelligence; it's a mysterious absorption of knowledge, requiring more than the usual frame and method. The point is made by Paul in his letter to the Galatians: "God has sent the spirit of his Son into our hearts" (Galatians 4:6). It's the three-part motion of the Trinity that we encounter in prayer, as the Word is revealed to us, meaning that we come fully or partially into contact with profound reality—another way of describing God.

The Lord's Prayer is justifiably popular, as with a bold stroke Jesus put prayer at the core of Christian living and offered an ideal model, one that (in my view) can simply be repeated or, better yet, used as a pattern for creative riffing. Here is the usual version (Matthew 6:9–14):

> Our father, which art in heaven,
> Hallowed be thy name.
> Thy kingdom come,
> Thy will be done in earth,
> As it is in heaven.
> Give us this day our daily bread.
> And forgive us our trespasses,
> As we forgive them that trespass against us.
> And lead us not into temptation,
> But deliver us from evil.
> For thine is the kingdom,
> The power, and the glory,
> For ever and ever.

Two versions of this prayer will be found, in Matthew and Luke, and the last three lines (the doxology) aren't always appended in early manuscripts. But the direction of the prayer remains straightforward. Jesus opens by praising God, regarded as a father—a traditional Jewish conception of God as head of the family. The Christian Trinity is, as noted above, a familial idea, a metaphor of relation that should feel comfortable to most people. He moves on to address the acceptance of God's kingdom, a spiritual kingdom in the process of emergence, with an explicit nod to the will of God, which implies giving up aspirations of control, of resting in God. This is key: letting go lies at the heart of all religious practice, which involves an acceptance of the nature of nature, the divine unfolding that is creation. If you truly accept this, all worries seem petty, insubstantial.

Jesus understands that God's will matters and that we don't get to determine how things fall out. Nonetheless, we often think of prayer as a "bid" for something, a request. And Jesus puts that into one big line when he ask for "daily bread"—an allusion to spiritual as well as physical food, or the daily needs that keep body and soul together. Then comes the forgiveness part, where Jesus suggests that we forgive those who harm us while acknowledging our own trespasses, places where we have stepped across the line, behaving badly, not taking into account the needs of others. That is, not treating others as we would wish to be treated ourselves.

This is a penitential prayer at heart, moving toward confession and repentance. We ask for mercy and hope to be spared from evil (in Greek, the "evil one" is *ho poneros*, a version of the Hebrew *ha'satan*). Evil is something we can't understand, and it's useful to anthropomorphize this abstract idea, to put all nastiness and vengefulness in a single skin: the Devil. Iniquity lies everywhere around us, and we hope that God will somehow allow us to step aside from this onrushing beast. "Deliver us from evil" is a powerful prayer moment.

One reason I love the Lord's Prayer is that it's the only time we really hear how Jesus sounded when he prayed. So we take on the mind of Christ by repeating these words, thus becoming, during the actual saying of the Lord's Prayer, not unlike Jesus himself. But, as noted above, one can simply use the Lord's Prayer as a basic pattern and elaborate in personal ways, moving from submission to God to celebration of his kingdom to requests for this or that to penitence and, ultimately, to an outward turning toward God in the doxology. The motion of this prayer, as with all meditation, is toward loving and praising God: "For thine is the kingdom, the power, and the glory." In this, we engage the affective will, a part of ourselves that we control, turning outward (or inward) to heaven, releasing our smaller selves to the larger Self.

There are many techniques for praying, and I will mention two of them that are special to me, part of my own practice, which involves praying the rosary and Centering Prayer. In a way, these represent opposite ends of the prayer spectrum, and yet they go well together; the former as preparation for the latter.

The rosary is a powerful prayer tool, a method of approaching God, of intermingling with the Creator, by digging into the silences around words, moving *through* words to a point of stillness. Prayer beads exist in most religious traditions, going back to Hindus in India in the third century BCE and perhaps before. They are simply a sequence of beads or knots in a rope that can be used for counting the number of prayers in a particular session. In the earliest days of Christianity, monks (as was the case with the Desert Fathers) frequently could not read. It was therefore difficult to keep track of one's devotions. The rosary was introduced as a way of keeping some account of progress during a round of prayer.

The Orthodox "prayer rope" is a version of the rosary, and it remains popular among Eastern monastics, those tracing their lineage back to Constantinople instead of Rome. They are usually made of black wool, with a varying number of knots, each of which represents the repetition of a particular prayer. Commonly the main prayer for each knot is the Jesus Prayer, which in its most traditional form goes like this: *Lord Jesus Christ, Son of God, have mercy on me, a sinner.* Traditionally this famous prayer dates to the fifth-century

158 ■ THE WAY OF JESUS

Greek ascetic Diadochos of Photiki. It has certainly traveled down the centuries, and it remains an evocative prayer that works well in repetitions.

The Roman tradition dates the praying of the rosary in its Marian form—dedicated to the mother of Jesus—from 1214, when (according to legend) it was given to Saint Dominic by Mary herself. The chief prayer that gets repeated is the famous Hail Mary (also called an Ave): *Hail Mary, full of grace, the Lord is with thee. Blessed art thou among women, and blessed is the fruit of thy womb, Jesus. Holy Mary, mother of God, pray for us sinners now and in the hour of our death.* I myself find this a hugely evocative prayer, and it forms the basis of my own practice, although the Roman Catholic version of the rosary is longer than the more recent Anglican version (which I employ), and it's more elaborately focused on the life of Christ.

It doesn't take much effort to learn how to pray the rosary in any version, and I would encourage anyone who finds this interesting to forge a personal practice, perhaps drawing on several traditions. The Roman version begins with crossing oneself, then saying the Apostle's Creed. This is followed by an Our Father (the Lord's Prayer), then three Hail Marys, which represents faith, hope, and love. Then comes what is called a Glory Be, a chant that goes like this: *Glory be to the Father, and to the Son, and to the Holy Spirit. As it was in the beginning, is now and ever shall be, world without end. Amen.* One then announces a mystery: there are twenty of them, such as an Angel of the Lord announcing to Mary that she will bear a child. As it were, the mysteries fall into four categories: joyful, luminous, sorrowful, and glorious. There are suggested patterns for various days of the week and seasons of the Church Year. An interlocking pattern of Hail Marys and Our Fathers follows, with an occasional Glory Be. Catholics end with a hymn to Mary that begins: *Hail, Holy Queen, Mother of mercy, our life, our sweetness, and our hope!*

The repetitions may seem monotonous, but they lead the person who prays into a kind of inward silence, where the chatter stops and one experiences the stillness of God. There are five "decades" in the rosary, each of these being a section where one repeats the Hail Mary ten times. So that's fifty times broken by a Glory Be. The idea that one should think about one of the holy mysteries while also saying a Hail Mary or reciting the Our Father or another chant seems awkward, even impossible, to some. I don't myself see that it's easily done, and for this reason I prefer the Anglican rosary, where the mind has more freedom to move in personal directions. I still use the Hail Mary as one of the main repetitions, sometimes alternating with the Jesus Prayer, which is also effective.

The Anglican rosary has only thirty-three beads, one for each year in the life of Jesus. There are seven beads in the "weeks," not ten, as in the Roman Catholic version. One begins with a welcoming or entrance bead, known as the invitatory bead. But first, as always in rosary prayers, one holds the cross and says something that casts an appropriate mood for prayer or contemplation. I like the Collect for Purity: *Almighty God, unto whom all hearts are open, all desires known, and from whom no secrets are hid: cleanse the thoughts of our hearts by the inspiration of the Holy Spirit, that we may perfectly love thee and worthily magnify thy holy name. Through Christ our Lord. Amen.* This is wonderfully cleansing, and it opens the heart to God. Then comes an Our Father. From this point you move in counterclockwise fashion through the four "decades," with seven shorter prayers, such as Hail Marys or the Jesus Prayer. The point is not to have to think about it. (I usually modify the last phrase from "hour of death" to "hour of our need," as we're not always thinking about our deaths; but there is hardly an hour that passes that is not an hour of need!)

The point of praying the rosary is to find the appropriate rhythm that allows for engaged contemplation and that opens the mind to God. The Anglican practice is less formalized, a gesture in the direction of rote prayer that is designed to liberate the conscious mind, to calm it; it directs one into deep realms of thought, into the wild freedom of non-thought, where one connects with love, with the divine center, with the source of all being, with whatever we mean by the word "God."

After finishing the rosary—or coming to a point in the round of prayer where I find myself ready to stop—I wait for a bit, perhaps five minutes, in silence, then move into a short period of what is called Centering Prayer, a method of prayerful meditation that has been quietly present in the Christian tradition for many centuries (going back to the Desert Fathers as well as *The Cloud of Unknowing*, a fourteenth-century classic of spirituality). This practice was brought to popular attention by Father Thomas Keating and others at a Trappist monastery in Massachusetts, and it has been usefully extended and reconsidered by others, including Cynthia Bourgeault, an Episcopal priest and theologian.

"Seek ye first the kingdom of God," Jesus said in Matthew 6:33. And where is that kingdom? "The Kingdom of God is within you," Jesus said in Luke 17:21. So the place to look for the kingdom is inside. And so the practice of Centering Prayer involves (according to Keating and his colleagues) a four-step process. First, one sits in a comfortable chair or on the floor. Feeling at ease in this seated position is essential. Then one chooses a word or phrase. This is your sacred word, and it might be something like Abba, which means "father" in Aramaic. Or a phrase such as "Come, Lord Jesus." The word or phrase should have personal resonance, and it's meant to open you up to the Divine Presence within. Third, you allow that word to float in your mind, but you don't think about anything in particular. Fourth, as your mind naturally reaches for other things—ideas, memories, subjects unrelated to your relationship with God—you bring your attention back to the personal word, gently, never forcing the issue. It's a process of releasing every thought or feeling, even the wish to connect to God. Just sit there and be yourself, in God.

There are obvious links between this method of prayer and various

Eastern forms of meditation. Transcendental Meditation is a recent movement founded by Maharishi Mahesh Yogi (1917–2008), an Indian sage who essentially revived an ancient Hindu practice wherein you focus on a unique mantra, allowing the mind to settle, repeating that word as necessary. The mind falls into a calm state by circling back to the mantra, or "sacred word." In Centering Prayer, one works to eliminate extraneous thoughts, to keep the mind still, quieting the random thought sparks and chatter that make up our mental life, for the most part, with its flickering thoughts, obsessive images, and a hyperfocus on certain things.

I can't see a problem here, though some Christians have been wary of using nontraditional or Eastern-leaning styles of prayer, as they seem awfully pagan, devoid of Christian content. But there is no reason that a Christian cannot use any technique of prayer or meditation in the quest for the "mind of Christ," the phrase that Saint Paul used so effectively. Christ-mind is what we seek: that space where we leave ourselves behind and connect to God through the *christos*, the mystical source of love in Jesus.

There is, of course, a strong correlation between breathing and any form of meditation or prayer. One of the simplest meditative practices involves simply coming back to one's breath. And the mantra, the word used in Centering Prayer, enables a kind of sacred breathing. Kabir, the fifteenth-century Indian poet and mystic, was asked by a student: "What is God?" He replied, "God is the breath inside the breath." He is also the Word inside the word. And silence remains the goal of meditation, an emptiness that leads to enlightenment, as Thoreau notes: "Silence is the communion of the conscious soul with itself." Elsewhere in his journals he writes:

> To be calm, to be serene! There is the calmness of the lake when there is not a breath of wind. . . . So it is with us. Sometimes we are clarified and calmed healthily, as we never were before in our lives, not by an opiate, but by

some unconscious obedience to the all-just laws, so that
we become like a still lake of purest crystal and without an
effort our depths are revealed to ourselves. All the world
goes by us and is reflected in our deeps. Such clarity![6]

There are many techniques associated with meditation and
prayer, which are closely allied. In its meditative form, prayer requires
intentionality: you lean into God, even upon him. You enter into a
state not unlike the Sanskrit idea of *shamatha*, which means "calm
abiding." You settle into the spirit of God, dive into the kingdom, allowing God-consciousness to arise naturally. It's a matter of attendance, in the literal sense of paying attention to what is there. It's
about listening to God, finding the voice that may well be the voice
of silence. One hopes to become "like a still lake of purest crystal,"
as Thoreau so beautifully put it; this is the condition of finding that
kingdom inside. It's a unification of the self with God, a putting on
the mind of Christ in a way that allows an awareness of the timeless
moment in time. Eternity opens.

It was right for Eliot to put prayer first in his list of five key practices, as it's the entry point into a relationship with God, especially the
God within, the source of all knowledge and being. But the Christian
life only begins inside, and it moves out into the world, step by step.
As Kierkegaard memorably said, "The function of prayer is not to influence God, but rather to change the nature of the one who prays."

▪ OBSERVANCE

Observance is about attending to outward forms, but doing so in
ways that enhance and define your approach to God. It is not a case
of mindlessly doing the right thing, such as turning up at church
on Sunday morning or observing the laws as put forward in the
Hebrew scriptures. In fact, what mainly separates Jesus from other

Jewish teachers of his time was the way he stressed that the time of just keeping the laws had passed, that more was required: an effort to love your neighbor and to create the beloved community, the emerging kingdom.

The Jewish people were bound by the Law, which is a rather complex term used to describe the Ten Commandments that Moses received from God on Mount Sinai, as described in Exodus 20:1–17. But there were 613 laws (*mitzvot*) that pious Jews discerned in the scriptures (and which are the subject of the Talmud); these regulations governed personal behavior, sexual practices, family matters, government, commerce, and civic life in general. There were laws about diet, slavery, tithing, cleanliness, and pretty much every aspect of human experience. Observance was meant to be strict, although various Jewish sects were more extreme than others: the Pharisees, for instance, were known for the zealous adherence to the laws in their minutest form.

Jesus himself is quoted on observance of the Law in various ways, and his behavior speaks volumes. Once he said, in response to someone questioning his view of the Law in Matthew 7:17–18, "Don't imagine I have come to abolish the Law or the Prophets; I haven't come to abolish them but to fulfill them. I speak the truth, that until heaven and earth disappear, not the smallest letter, not the least stroke of a pen, will be ignored from the Law until everything is accomplished." But this is somewhat misleading, as Jesus and his disciples showed a certain cavalier attitude toward some of the laws.

Jesus and his disciples didn't, for example, think one should necessarily avoid work on the Sabbath (Matthew 12:1–14). They didn't worry too much about ritual washing before a meal, and would sit down and eat with those who were not Jewish (Matthew 15:1–2). Their dietary rules were not nearly as strict as those kept by more pious Jews (Mark 7:1–23). So perhaps one could argue that Jesus understood that the situation mattered, and one should remain flexible in interpreting the Law. He put people first, and invariably said that love was what counted most: loving God as well as loving one's neighbor as oneself.

There was some disagreement among those following the Way of Jesus about what exactly "following the Law" meant. The Jerusalem co-hort, led by James (the brother of Jesus) and Peter, were strict Jews who considered the Law still inviolable. A decade or more after the death of Jesus, Paul himself met in Jerusalem with James, Peter, Barnabas, and others (Acts 15:1–29). One point of contention was the so-called God-fearers, or Gentiles who wished to join the Way. Following the lead of Paul (who had been trained as a Pharisee), it was decided af-ter much discussion and argument that as long as people were "in Christ," which means that they had done what Paul suggested and "put on the mind of Christ," they should not have to abide by the strict observance of Jewish law. (Crucially, this meant that male God-fearers didn't have to undergo circumcision: a big relief for many!)

This lessening of restrictions for Gentiles played a role in spread-ing the faith throughout the Roman Empire and beyond. Paul, like Jesus himself, would share a meal with anyone. He wrote often about the law, in fact, in his letters to the Galatians and the Romans; but his views were inconsistent. Perhaps like most sophisticated Jews at the time, he regarded the Law as a gift from God, a sign of his in-timacy with his people, a gesture of love and concern; but as often happens when literalism takes hold, a certain doggedness set in. Paul felt that one could not gain enlightenment through obedience alone; but there was much to admire in the Law, which had meant so much to the people of Israel, as "the glory was theirs and the covenants; to them were given the Law and the worship of God and his promises" (Romans 9.4).

Christians have dealt with the idea of the Law in various ways, and attitudes toward it have shifted throughout the centuries, espe-cially after the Reformation and beyond, when (as often in Protestant circles) "the Law" was identified with Roman Catholic insistence on strict observance of certain rules (often derided: such as the practice, once common among Catholics, of not eating meat on Fridays). As they would, people often find a version of the Law that suits them, as Auden suggests in his memorable "Law Like Love," a poem in which he concludes that law is like love in that it has no deep explanation ("Like love we don't know where or why") and is difficult to sustain ("Like love we seldom keep"); and yet we acknowledge that there are laws, if not a grand abstraction: the Law.

I often turn in my mind to Eliot as an exemplary Christian, one who found a way of integrating his faith into his life and its daily rituals. In middle age, he became a warden of St. Stephen's Church in Kensington, the part of London where he lived for decades. I once visited that church with Mrs. Eliot, who recalled that Eliot had stopped there almost daily, deeply aware of the importance of observance. He also went on regular retreats. Indeed, "Little Gidding" (the last of the *Four Quartets*) was inspired by a visit to a small Anglican religious community founded at this site outside Cambridge in the early seventeenth century by Nicholas Ferrar. This was a high church community, devoted to the Anglican Book of Common Prayer and religious rituals, such as the Liturgy of the Hours, in which the hours of the day were marked by set prayers.

The question remains, however: is observance necessary for the Christian life? And by this I mean: do you really "have" to go to church or participate in rituals throughout the year, as during Lent, with its many special services, its suggestion of fasting and other practices? I believe the answer is yes. Mere mortals need Holy Communion, need to gather around an altar, to worship together, to praise God, to see themselves as part of a larger body, what is often called the "body of Christ." Public prayer, communal confession, sharing the sacred meal: these are parts of the pattern, but they are useful as well as inspiring. And the observance of holidays—feast days, high holy days—seems worthy as well, as this kind of observance keeps us fastened to the faith, lit up by its brighter moments, moving along the affirming grooves of the Church Year.

It's so easy to fall away, to lose oneself in the distractions and ob-
sessions that lay siege to our minds, scattering our attention in countless directions. In "Burnt Norton," Eliot observed the commuters in
London with their "time-ridden faces / Distracted from distraction by
distraction." And let me be frank here: *this is me much of the time*. It's
probably all of us. Living as we do in a largely secular world, with so
many shiny objects straining to grab our attention, we effortlessly slip
into a state of emptiness in which we react to whatever shimmers or
shrieks past us on the screen, or as we walk in the streets, or try to fall
asleep. Our monkey minds hop around, undisciplined, chattering. We
can't settle, and in our distraction and confusion, the possibilities for
finding God seem few and far between.

So we need observance, which functions to bring us back to ourselves, back to the possibilities of the spirit, back to God. There is
much to be said for holding the space, for keeping the practice in an
active and intentional way, allowing for the mysteries of the faith to
work as they will. Without regular attendance to ritual and practice,
there is less likelihood that those "hints and guesses" that direct us
toward enlightenment will occur.

There is an interesting analogy with writing here. Poets, for instance, are often asked about inspiration. This can arise out of nowhere. But if the poet isn't willing to sit at his or her desk for long
hours, in a regular way, it seems less than likely that inspiration will
occur. "Poetry is not only dream and vision; it is the skeleton archi-
tecture of our lives," writes Audre Lorde, herself a luminous poet. "It
lays the foundations for a future of change, a bridge across our fears of
what has never been before."[7] If you put in the word "religion" where
you see "poetry" in this evocative formulation, it becomes clear that
the two have much in common. Religious practice becomes, in the
rituals of observance, as in habits of daily practice, "the skeleton ar-
chitecture of our lives." And it also lays the foundations for transformation, "a bridge across our fears" into a land of quiet, clarity, and
connection to God.

▪ DISCIPLINE

Observance requires discipline, which is in effect a widening of the notion of observance. Eliot was himself a disciplined man who adapted at a fairly early age to life in a bank, with its long hours and the obvious pressures of conformity. He dressed for work and went to the office year after year. In later years, he would spend the afternoon at Faber, the publishing house where he worked for decades, editing a wide range of modern authors, including Auden and his old friend Ezra Pound. As a writer, he understood the discipline of tradition, going back to Aristotle, Horace, and Quintilian, each of whom noted how tradition itself channels us in potentially useful and creative directions.

By 1927, Eliot had come to embrace the Anglo-Catholic vein of Christianity, as he thought that enlightenment (or "salvation," the usual Latinized translation from the Greek *soteria*, which occurs forty-six times in the New Testament) might come only within the practices of a sturdy tradition, which helps to hold the space where inspiration occurs. In 1951, in a memorable preface to an anthology of meditative writing, he wrote that "no man has ever climbed to the higher stages of the spiritual life, who has not been a believer in a particular religion or at least a particular philosophy."[8] In "Religion Without Humanism," written in 1930, he said that the "difficult discipline" is the "discipline and training of emotion," adding that he had "only found this through dogmatic religion."[9] In a 1932 commentary that appeared in the *Criterion*, a journal that he edited, he spoke of "the discipline of an exact religious faith."[10]

I would suggest that Eliot is not mounting an argument for theological rigidity, although it can sound like that. The mere fact that he alludes to a broad range of religions in *Four Quartets* (as in his other poetry) implies that he valued a variety of spiritual traditions, including Hinduism and Buddhism, which had both been attractive to him throughout his life. In "East Coker," he speaks of poetry as a "raid on the inarticulate," and I would venture that, for him, religious practice was conducive to this raiding. Eliot understood that discipline was required in both writing and faith, and that without a firm grip on what went before, the accumulation of words, deeds, and habits stretching deep into the past, one could not really create in the moment.

Poetry and spirituality mingled in Eliot's work. In an essay on Jacques Maritain, he observed that if poetry is not to become "a lifeless repetition of forms," then the poet must explore "the frontiers of spirit." He added, cautiously: "The frontiers of spirit are more like the jungle which, unless continuously kept under control, is always ready to encroach and eventually obliterate the cultivated area."[11] So the discipline he refers to in "The Dry Salvages" involves more than mere repetition, as in liturgical repetitions, although Eliot as a poet and Anglo-Catholic loved repetitions and refrains, which have been a key part of religious services and practices throughout the centuries. But he remained highly aware of the possibility that one's practice—in either poetry or religion—could sink into "a lifeless repetition."

One reads in the second letter of Timothy (2 Timothy 1:7) that "God has not given us a spirit of timidity but of power, love, and self-discipline." "Discipline yourself for the purpose of godliness," says the author of Timothy (1 Timothy 4:7). But what does this really mean, to find this sense of discipline—or self-discipline?

Discipline can take many forms. I once sat with Buddhist monks in the Swayambhunath "Monkey Temple" in Kathmandu throughout a long afternoon of chanting, stunned by the visceral power of group prayer, with its sonorous repetitions, experiencing the sense of an entire group lifted by the spirit. I've seen the long rows of devout Muslims in their daily prayers in Egypt, Jordan, Turkey, Morocco, and elsewhere. They enter into the presence of God at appointed intervals, and the spirit permeates their lives. I've also watched orthodox Jews praying at the Wailing Wall in Jerusalem or in their prayer halls in Mea She'arim, one of the oldest neighborhoods in Jerusalem. My own experience of travel, and making contact with other religious traditions, has only reinforced my sense of what spiritual discipline means.

"Discipline" and "disciple" share the same Greek root word (*mathetes*), for one who is apprenticed to a master. In the ancient world, all teaching was apprenticeship, with the model of somebody being attached to an expert, usually a craftsman. At the time of Jesus, the term almost always referred to one who wished to learn and therefore adhered to the pattern of the teacher in joyous replication. And so Rabbi Jesus is somebody who "disciplines" us, invites us to follow a pattern, behave consciously in certain ways, being kind and responsive to the needs of others, alert to the motions of the spirit, willing to extend oneself. Personal discipleship was common within the Greek and Jewish worlds in the first century and before, and it extended to those who followed a particular master. Jesus called those around him into discipleship (Mark 3:14). "A disciple is not greater than his teacher," Luke says, "but everyone who is fully trained by him will become like him" (Luke 6:40).

A disciple, then, is someone committed to the master, to discipline itself as a mode of learning, and this involves self-regulation: consciously focusing on the practice of faith as taught by Jesus and the traditions of Christian living. It involves saving time in a structured way for prayer or meditation, attending services throughout the Church Year, paying close attention to the contours of the progress through Advent and Lent, Easter, and beyond. It means developing a practice of reading the scriptures: monks, for example, will read the Bible (especially the psalms) with a keen focus, allowing the language to dig into the mind and gather resonance and meaning (a systematic practice known as *lectio divina*—a kind of prayerful close reading in which one moves from a literal to a figurative understanding of the text).

Discipline means giving oneself to something or someone in love and hope. In Proverbs 12:1 we read: "Whoever loves discipline, loves knowledge." We learn a craft by apprenticing ourselves to someone proficient in that craft. In many ways we surrender to God, especially to the God within us, as a way of losing our attachment to our smaller selves, our petty understanding of what life is about. And this discipline can take many forms.

When Paul spoke of discipline, as he did in 2 Corinthians 7:1, he asked those who followed the Way of Jesus to purify themselves by disallowing "everything that contaminates body and spirit." In conservative or fundamentalist traditions, this often means abstaining from alcohol and sex. I would caution against that kind of discipline, which seems to me anti-life. There is nothing wrong with either drinking or sex, although each of these activities requires discipline. One should drink in moderation, as it's unhealthy to get drunk, and it's also dangerous, especially when it puts others in peril (as when intoxicated people drive). Sexuality requires rigorous discipline, too: it's never wise to allow one's impulses to overwhelm common sense. And marriage, too, is part of that discipline.

Wendell Berry, one of my favorite American writers, has aptly compared marriage to poetry, and he has talked about the discipline of marriage in fruitful ways. In "The Body and the Earth," he writes: "What marriage offers—and what fidelity is meant to protect—is the possibility of moments when what we have chosen and what we desire are the same. Such a convergence obviously cannot be continuous. No relationship can continue for long at its highest emotional pitch. But fidelity prepares us for the return of these moments, which give us the highest joy we can know; that of union, communion, atonement (in the root sense of at-one-ment)."[12] Elsewhere, he notes that poetry and marriage both depend upon given forms, on traditions and the conventions that operate within them.

There are many forms of discipline, and marriage is only one of them. But each of these implies a dependence on certain forms, even norms. There is a communal aspect to this discipline as well, as one responds to others besides oneself in all forms of discipline, including prayer and observance, working for the benefit of the community of faith in addition to one's own enlightenment. Conventions lead to liberation, to freedom, when practiced with love. Prayer, for instance, is rarely a single voice; one joins with others, in church, in public, confessing sins or beseeching God in some way. The community finds itself in this form of prayer, finds its voice. (I like the notion of *bodhichitta*, elaborated on within the discourse of Mahayana Buddhism, where we learn that we must look beyond our own liberation to consider the welfare of the larger community, seeking the enlightenment of others and finding ourselves within that process.) Prayer as a pathway to enlightenment includes individual and communal prayer, and these will usually overlap.

Prayer is not the only form of discipline; but it's a beginning, and it starts with daily efforts to understand or intuit the actions required to grow in God's love. We bend to the contours of faith or trust (*pistos*), recalling the wise words of Jesus, who said: "Whoever is able to trust in little ways will learn to trust in larger matters" (Luke 16:10). Discipline moves from narrow to wider arenas of our lives, as we adhere to the shapes and formal patterns of the Way of Jesus, becoming disciples or learners, trying out what he suggests. Discipline helps us to create spaces where we encounter the spirit, allowing it to fill us, to buoy us, as we move toward his kingdom.

▪ THOUGHT

The counterbalance to lifeless or rote repetition is creative thought. As a poet, Eliot believed in "the direct sensuous apprehension of thought," as noted in "The Metaphysical Poets." He wished to cultivate the union of thought and feeling—to the point where the one became the other. This fusion (in Eliot's mind represented by the poetry of John Donne) represents a drive toward integration, or wholeness, and it requires conscious effort. I like to imagine that, in prayer, in church, while reading scripture or poetry, Eliot himself worked to turn his abstract and disembodied thoughts into feelings—a process of apprehension, the accession of sensory experience in ways that transcend mundane realities, gaining access to those "spots of time" that Wordsworth wrote about. It was all about a drive toward the deep center of human consciousness

This center is a version of the Greek *logos*, the underlying intelligibility of the world, the shaping vision that underlies all consciousness: a philosophical version of the unified field theory that has obsessed physicists in our time. Eliot's thought drives us toward this unified field of consciousness, toward the Word, or *logos*, that was there at the beginning—as in the opening lines of John's Gospel, where we read: "In the beginning was the Word, and the Word was with God, and the Word was God." But it takes some effort to come into a disciplined relationship with this center, and part of that discipline is the work of knowledge.

Again, Eliot is a model here: a man perpetually in search of knowledge about the world, a learned reader and writer who cast a broad intellectual net, finding parallels and associations in unlikely places. In "East Coker," the poet-speaker tells himself: "I said to my soul, be still." (This echoes the famous line in Psalm 46: "Be still and know that I am God.") And that stillness involves waiting; indeed, "the faith and the love and the hope are all in the waiting." Eliot says firmly, talking more to himself than his readers: "Wait without thought, for you are not ready for thought." This is an acute description of meditation: waiting, allowing consciousness to fill slowly, moving toward what Eliot calls "the stillness the dancing." This is the "still point of the turning world." It's the seeking for God in waiting, waiting for thought—but thought isn't absent or avoided. It comes before and after the stillness. It prepares the ground for the center, just as reading and thinking prepare the ground for the possibility of a complex apprehension of reality.

But how much should a Christian, someone following the Way of Jesus, know? Didn't Jesus actually tell us to come to him as little children, and therefore without much experience or knowledge of the world? I suspect that we're looking at different levels of thought and feeling here: the childlike innocence that allows us to take in fresh learning and avoid stifling assumptions can only be helpful in making contact with divine realities. God did endow us with minds, with the ability to reason and learn, so it seems likely that the careful and disciplined use of our intelligence is a good thing. Simplemindedness and simplicity are miles apart. In fact, some of the best Christian thinkers have been quite bold in the ferocity and breadth of their work.

As noted above, I was shocked when, as a college freshman, I encountered for the first time the writings of Tillich and Bultmann, for instance, two German theologians who had moved far beyond the simplistic Christianity of my childhood. They drew me toward the synoptic study of the Gospels, looking at them "together" (*syn-optic*). When you compare the Christmas stories in Matthew and Luke, for instance, you see that they draw on different sources, and these two stories are incompatible if taken literally. One could race through the scriptures and find literal contradictions on every page. But that only reflects the nature of their composition, and—given the right attitude—it invites us to read these texts with greater openness to symbolic meanings.

My own sense is that the more one knows, the more one wants to know. Faith and knowledge are not on a collision course; one can't have a mature and complex faith without a substantial body of knowledge at one's command, including an awareness of the textual history of the scriptures and a broad sense of historical Christianity, its evolution over the centuries. If you follow the Way of Jesus, you should have a basic grasp of Judaism, Hinduism, Buddhism, and Islam: elements of these interact with Christianity in crucial ways that can be ignored only at the risk of an ignorance that is hardly bliss. It's quite dangerous to think that *only* the Way of Jesus opens toward the center, toward God. As Ikkyu, the fifteenth-century Zen poet, wrote: "Many paths lead up the mountain, but at the top we all observe the same bright moon." Anyone who spends time with devout followers of other paths will know the truth of this, and it will not stifle one's Christian views but allow them to breathe in a richer context.

An awareness of the history of the New Testament, its composition and sources (which do affect its meaning), seems essential to anyone's growth in the faith. Few of the Christians I met in my early years as a Baptist even knew that Paul's letters were the first Christian texts, for instance, or that only seven of them were actually written by Paul, whereas there was a "school of Paul" responsible for the rest. It helps to know something about this. And some knowledge of the Gnostic gospels is useful, too: they provide angles on Jesus and his teachings not available in the canonic Gospels. In truth, I don't think one can ever know enough, although one should take a cautious approach, gathering information as best one can, learning to sort good information from bad, picking one's way through the underbrush of pseudoscholarly chatter that obscures the path to understanding. There is a complicated process of discernment here, and one needs the active energies of the Holy Spirit to make this work possible.

I have such strong memories of my father in the early years after he experienced his conversion to Christianity. He was in his late thirties, not well-educated: he never finished high school, nor had he developed a taste for reading. But he set about studying the Bible with an intensity I found impressive. Every morning he rose early, at least two hours before the rest of the family. He went down into the living room, where he had established a place at the end of the couch with a side table filled with biblical commentaries and, of course, his own Bible. He read the books of the Bible in order, from beginning to end, keeping notes, and when he was finished he started again. It was a lifelong project for him, and one that he followed until his death in his mid-eighties. He also attended evening classes in the Bible once or twice a week, as well as study sessions at his church. Quite sensibly he believed that anyone following the Way of Jesus needed to know as much as possible about the textual record of Christianity.

I have found that reading is more than useful: it's crucial to maintaining one's faith. This means reading the Bible, but it's also important to read widely in various (even contradictory) theological veins. I have my own preferred theologians at the moment, including Rowan Williams, Richard Rohr, and Cynthia Bourgeault. The philosopher Charles Taylor is rarely far from my thoughts. I try not to lose contact with shaping figures in my intellectual life such as Buber, Barth, Tillich, Teilhard de Chardin, Hans Kung, and many others. And I find myself discovering new and arresting voices each year, as recently I encountered the work of Douglas A. Campbell, a Pauline scholar and professor of the New Testament at Duke Divinity School.

Writing to the Philippians (4:8), Paul said, "At last, brothers and sisters, take to heart whatever is true, is worthy of respect, is just, is pure, whatever is lovely, is commendable. Take to heart whatever is excellent or worthy of praise. And study these things." Indeed, there is no limit to what you can learn, and each Christian must follow his or her own path of knowledge, moving with care through the material at hand, learning about the traditions of Christian thought, experiencing Christian art (poetry, painting, music), and positioning this knowledge within other religious and secular traditions, as they are not wholly separate but entwined with them.

■   ACTION

The final point in Eliot's prescription for Christian practice is action. One thinks of the letter of James (2:17): "Faith by itself, if not accompanied by action, is dead." Indeed, the main goal of the Way of Jesus is not personal salvation (although that matters) but social justice: the Kingdom of God appearing in our midst.

This isn't just a Christian mission, although it follows naturally from a vision of Christ. I often draw parallels between Christianity and Buddhism, and think especially of the Eightfold Path, which directs us out of the absorbing (and suffocating) cycles of life and death.

This path (which could be Christian as well as Buddhist) involves Right Understanding, Right Intention, Right Speech, Right Action, Right Livelihood, Right Effort, Right Mindfulness, and Right Concentration. These are all forms of action: moving in the world toward awareness, reaching outward, extending one's gratitude to the whole world to whatever extent is possible, bringing all of one's talents to bear for the creation of the Kingdom of God.

In Judaism, there is a great phrase that represents a call to action: *tikkun olam*, which means "to repair the world." That was a tenet of mystical Judaism, going back to the Mishnaic period in the second century CE; but those involved with the Kabbala (in the Middle Ages) found it especially alluring and developed this notion, which in modern times has been further interpreted to mean establishing or extending God's qualities—especially his mercy and sense of justice—throughout the world. As Jill Jacobs has written in a review of the concept: "This phrase is fascinating both in its endurance and in its capacity to change meanings according to the needs of the hour."[13] *Tikkun olam* opens us to those around us, especially those in need of our sympathy or love, our money, our presence.

The Way of Jesus also involves making choices about how we live among our neighbors. Do we treat them like ourselves? Do we discover and love God in our neighbors, which is probably the only way one can indeed discover and love God, as the Desert Fathers taught? It is useful to keep in mind what Jesus said on this subject (Matthew 25:40): "What you do to the least person in the world, you do to me." The question of how to treat others, especially those on the margins of society, weighs heavily on those who wish to imitate Christ, to find that generous and merciful place in our own hearts where God lives.

One can, in fact, read the entire Sermon on the Mount as a theoretical guide to right action. It's also a discourse on *karma*, at least in the idea that whatever one sows, one eventually reaps. In a larger sense, the entire life of Christ might be taken as a guide to right action, a call to ethical behavior. Jesus didn't simply say that we should love our neighbors as ourselves; he showed us how to accomplish this in an exemplary fashion. He focused on the poor, those whom he called "blessed" in the Beatitudes. He lived communally with his disciples, sharing meals, praying, putting into practice ideals that arose in the process of thought. He had no pretensions, and sought the company of those on the margins: prostitutes, beggars, the lame, the mentally ill, the hungry. He sat with lepers. He knelt and prayed with anyone, regardless of their class or gender, nationality or religious affiliation. And his offhand remarks, as recorded in the Gospels, are full of calls to action, as in Matthew 7:20: "By their fruits you will know them." Perhaps the most vivid passage about the Christian call to action comes from James: 2:14–17: "What good is it, my brothers, if somebody says he has faith but does not have right action? Can his faith save him? If a brother or sister is poorly clothed and lacking in daily food, and one of you says to them, 'Go in peace, be warmed and filled,' without giving them the things needed for the body, what good is that? So faith by itself, if it does not have works as well, is dead." In short, faith demands a grounding in action: "Let us not live in word and talk but in deed and truth" (1 John 3:18).

From the earliest times, Christians set out to change society for the better, to right wrongs, to help those in need. I often think of Saint Telemachus, from the late fourth century, a monk from the East who came to Rome to protest the barbaric practice of gladiatorial contests (according to the historian Theodoret, the Bishop of Cyrrhus in Syria). He thrust himself into the arena at one of these horrific contests and was butchered as the bloodthirsty crowd cheered on his attackers. But word of his protest reached the emperor, Honorius, who took it upon himself to ban these fights. This legend of a good man willing to lose his life in order to protest a cruel form of entertainment has often been retold (in different versions), and it remains inspiring.

Examples abound in history of Christians willing to put themselves on the line for a good cause. One thinks, for instance, of

William Wilberforce, the eloquent British politician from the nineteenth century, who stood firmly behind the Abolition of Slavery Act, which was passed—after endless attempts by Wilberforce and others—in 1833. His speeches were impassioned, fueled by his fervent belief in the teachings of Jesus, and he never gave up until (just three days before his death) this bill passed, a milestone in the abolitionist movement. In one of his memorable speeches (1789), he detailed the horrors of the slave trade, ending with these chilling words: "Having heard all of this you may choose to look the other way but you can never again say that you did not know."

Most churches try to help those in need, regarding this as key to their mission. My own church, for instance, is St. Stephens in Vermont, and each year we hold a charity bazaar in the summer called Peasant Market, where we raise a good deal of money that is given away to local charities, such as local homeless shelters and mental health facilities. We try to feed the hungry in our part of Vermont with free weekly meals. This is hardly exceptional; it's quite typical of churches, which in so many ways contribute to helping the poor and needy with food, clothing, and shelter. But is this enough?

I think of the great Dorothy Day (1897–1980), a cofounder (with Peter Maurin) of the Catholic Worker Movement, which opened chapter houses across the country during the height of the Great Depression. They provided food and shelter to the poorest of the poor while protesting on their behalf wherever they could. Day was an early suffragist as well, going to prison in 1917 on behalf of the right for women to vote. She was a prolific writer who used her pen to argue for social justice, peace, and civil rights—her work as editor of The Catholic Worker stretched from 1933 until her death. She was a strong voice for pacifism as well, often citing the words of Jesus: "Put away your sword, for whoever lives by the sword shall die by the sword."

Jesus was an advocate for nonviolence, as portrayed in the Gospels, although he could show righteous anger when it was needed, as when he overturned the tables of money changers in Herod's Temple only days before his execution. He famously preached that one should "turn the other cheek" against those who strike you, in Matthew 5:39. And this strong teaching has inspired writers and activists such as Thoreau, Tolstoy, Gandhi, and King. Indeed, on September 7, 1910—shortly before his death—Tolstoy wrote to the young Gandhi, who was then engaged in acts of nonviolent resistance in South Africa, that Jesus himself "knew, as all reasonable men must do, that any employment of force is incompatible with love as the highest law of life." He argued that in Christianity the "law of love has been more clearly and definitely given than in any other religion" and that it was therefore incumbent upon all who followed the Way of Jesus to act in a nonviolent way.

In his later decades, Tolstoy devoted himself to helping those in need, such as when in 1895 he began to work with others to help a persecuted minority, the Doukhobors, persuading the government to allow them to immigrate to Canada. He sided again and again with the poor and with those subjected to the persecution of the Tsarist government. In what might be called his love-based activism, he became a vegetarian—he did not want animals to suffer. And he used his astonishing fame, in Russia and throughout the world, to campaign on behalf of human rights wherever he found these abused. He was as well a ferocious opponent of capital punishment. "I cannot be silent," he said, in the face of hangings, which were common in Russia and around the world at the time.

One has seen various attempt to interpret Christian "action" on the left and right. On the left there was (and continues to be) a movement in Latin America known as liberation theology, which began in 1968 in Colombia, when a group of bishops put forward a document that affirmed the rights of the poor and charged industrialized countries with putting profits ahead of people. A *Theology of Liberation*, by Gustavo Gutiérrez, a Peruvian priest and scholar, came out in 1971, and soon a number of high-profile leaders joined in this movement, including Archbishop Oscar Romero of El Salvador. Leonardo Boff, a

Franciscan-trained theologian from Brazil, added substantially to the movement with a withering critique of American power and its negative effects in the world, although he was driven from the church, especially over his views on the church itself, as in his *Church: Charism and Power* (1985), a look at liberation theology and its relationship to the established church.

Some within the liberation theology movement argued that God speaks through the poor, and that Christianity must be centered on helping them find their voice. These liberation theologists traced the theological underpinnings of this view back to the Hebrew and Christian scriptures, looking for ways to improve the lives of those on the margins of Latin American society. Setting up "base communities" of Christians in local areas, they sought to help the poor improve their diets and get clean water, medical help, proper sewage and electricity, and other essential needs. Needless to say, elites in various Latin American countries, and within the hierarchy of the church itself, worried that this kind of thinking (and behavior) had a Marxist tinge, and in the nineties the Vatican itself sought to limit the impact of this movement.

On the right-leaning side, there has been a consistent movement among Roman Catholics and evangelical Christians to put an end to abortion. This broad-based movement took political shape in the early seventies, after the US Supreme Court's *Roe v. Wade* ruling in 1973. Of course the argument for or against "life" turns on one's notion of when life begins: at the moment of conception or, as more traditionally, at the moment of birth. It's the nature of this gestation period that has confounded this issue for many. When, indeed, does the soul inhabit the body? Should anyone really draw such a line between body and soul? These are good questions, and they demand prayerful answers. I would simply note that many of those who decry abortion at any stage in gestation are quite silent on the matter of executing criminals. I have a deep personal antipathy to capital punishment, which should certainly be part of any dialogue about the right to life. (Executions are barbarous, and should have no place in a civilized world or just society. Jesus himself suggested as much when, in the Sermon on the Mount, he overturned the old idea of "an eye for an eye." An eye for an eye only leads to societal blindness on a massive scale, and moral bankruptcy.)

In fact, those following Jesus and his example can find many ways to put their values into practice, imitating the life of Christ in daily practices. For me, one of the central features of Christian living is a reverence for the planet God has created. We were given a perfect world, mythically represented as the Garden of Eden. With our foolish sense of "progress," we destroyed what we had, fouling our rivers and seas, killing countless species of animal and plant life, drawing upon us floods and fires: the real-world consequences of global warming that affect and afflict us all, everywhere on the planet. This "progress" was a form of eating from the Tree of the Knowledge of Good and Evil. As in the *mythos*, we were duly sent into the fallen world to farm, to hunt and gather, to find community and sustain it. The directions could not have been clearer: "Teach us to number our days well, that we may cultivate a heart of wisdom," we read in Psalm 90:12. This means finding ways to live as stewards of the environment. It means pushing our governments, and our communities, toward stewardship as well, as suggested by Pope Francis in *Laudato si*, his eloquent encyclical of 2016.

Francis has understood that climate change brings terrible harm to the poor, and it fuels a destructive cycle that will lead to the impoverishment of our good earth. We have, as the pontiff says, turned our sacred planet into a "polluted wasteland full of debris, desolation and filth." It was astonishing to see this language coming from the Vatican, but here it is: a call to action that includes reducing waste, planting trees, separating rubbish into things that can and cannot be recycled, driving less, and many other simple practical forms of action. Francis asks us to "resolve to live differently," with a full awareness that "the earth is the Lord's." He sees the destruction of our environment through global warming as nothing less than sinful. In effect, the pope put forward a religious case for creating a sustainable economy and waging war on climate change. This fits the call for "right action," and it's quite specific.

Right action, then, invites all of us who follow the Way of Jesus to lead an ethical life conceived in terms that seem broadly consistent in all the world's religions, and this involves *doing* things: protesting wrongs and, in one's daily life, behaving in ethical ways to promote social justice. The elements of these forms of action are evident in the Eightfold Path as well as in the Ten Commandments and the Sermon on the Mount, which reformulates, redefines, and extends the Law of Moses. As we read in Psalm 33:5: "The Lord loves right action and justice; the earth is full of his unfailing love." (I have translated the word *tsaddik*, in Hebrew, as "right action." It occurs 206 times in the Old Testament, and in contexts that support this interpretation.)

The Gospels themselves are full of examples of Jesus talking about the need for social justice, for right action, and instances where he models this behavior. He speaks up for those whom society at large often denigrates and punishes. "He has anointed me to bring the Good News to the poor, and sent to proclaim that captives will be released, that the blind will see, that the oppressed will be set free," Jesus says in Luke 4:18–19. One can't imagine any clearer message. But of course this sort of right action demands a great deal from us. It requires us to will ourselves to do the right thing, however difficult at times.

Carl Jung once suggested that "right action comes from right thinking" and there is "no cure and no improving the world that does not begin with the individual himself." This means discernment: knowing the right thing to do, which must vary from time to time and from person to person. It may mean attending a protest against fracking or signing a petition on climate change. It may simply mean choosing to recycle, being aware that the earth is precious and that resources are scarce, and the individual duty to behave properly when no one is looking is important. It may require us to write a check to a homeless shelter or campaign for a particular candidate for political office. It may draw us to march in a gay pride parade. It could easily mean visiting the sick or someone in prison. The possibilities for right action are countless.

One obeys God because one discerns that this is the right thing to do. And discernment is perhaps the first part of action. It means being awake to what happens in the world, as noted in 1 John 3:17–18: "If anyone has material possessions and sees a brother or sister in need but has no pity on them, how can the love of God be in that person? Dear children, let us not love with words or speech but with actions and in truth."

In *Four Quartets*, especially in the fifth section of "The Dry Salvages," Eliot offers this pattern for Christian living that I've used as a guide here, asking us to think about prayer, observance, discipline, thought, and action in fresh ways. In "Little Gidding," which brings his long sequence to a conclusion, he invites us to kneel "where prayer has been valid." This is, at least to me, inspirational, and prayer in this sense becomes a form of action.

The fact is, the Way of Jesus is more about practical living than abstract theory, however much we try to ground our actions in understanding. This point was made by Aquinas, who said, *Prius vita quam doctrina*. That is, life comes before doctrine. And life is what breaks moment by moment, inviting us to make choices. It's our past as well as our present, and our intentions for the future as well: how we pitch ourselves into the work at hand while trying to discern the motions of the spirit within our souls. That Christianity provides guidelines for this work has always been part of its success in the world: one simply imitates Jesus, who behaved in a perfect way. In modeling our life on his, we may at times find ourselves at a loss, wondering if what we're doing makes any sense. But it's worth remembering the words of Thomas à Kempis from *The Imitation of Christ*: "God can do more than human beings can understand."

CONCLUSION

The Way of Jesus is, then, about a way of life. It's about living in the joy of the Resurrection, which is not a one-time affair but a process of continuous rebirth. This rebirth happens now, not tomorrow. And its perpetual bubbling up obliterates the fear of death, which brings a natural end to clock time, the minute-by-minute madness of our daily lives.

I've found this all quite liberating as a way of being in the world, with its attachment to a challenging but wonderfully detailed pattern for living. *Love God and love your neighbor as yourself*: those are the two large commandments of Jesus, and each directive requires work. Loving God means getting to know God, and I've found that this is possible in only two ways. The first is through prayer and meditation, a time each day when I let the voice of God arise within me, when I feel its direction, adhere to rhythms of thought that I find both soothing and bracing, this bedrock reality where I can genuinely rest in God. And then there is the hard work of loving our neighbors as ourselves.

Quite often I don't like my neighbors, or—if I do—it's immensely difficult to extend myself in ways that show (or create) my love for them. Mostly I don't even know my neighbors, but I have over time grown increasingly sensitive to those in my community who are suffering: the hungry and poor, those who feel disenfranchised, put

184

down. I'm no saint, believe me. It's hard for me to put myself out for other people. But with the help of my faith community, I've been able to extend myself, and this hard work lifts me up. "Cast your bread upon the waters," we read in the beautiful eleventh chapter of Ecclesiastes, "for you shall find it after many days." I've discovered in my own life that the practice of generosity is worth cultivating. Give it all away: your heart and soul, whatever money you can spare, but—mainly—your sympathy. This means thinking about ways to enhance the lives of those in your community who are suffering and those well beyond it.

The world ripples with pain, injustices, indifference to needs both large and small. But God speaks in many voices, always finding a local accent, often clinging to myths and traditions with a local inflection, and this is as it should be. In my own life, he has spoken through Jesus, who repeatedly said that the poor and meek shall inherit the earth, and that the last shall be first. He has invited us to sit down with total strangers, whores, tax collectors, felons, and those with incurable and perhaps contagious diseases. He says that if a man wants our shirt, we should give him our coat as well. He has urged us to behave like insane people and turn the other cheek when struck, assuring us that the way of love is difficult, perhaps mad, but suggesting that it's the only way to heal a broken world.

Some Christians, misreading their scriptures, have cast the poor in a bad light, imagining it's somehow their fault that poverty or illness or injustice has befallen them. We live, however, in a ferociously class-bound and narrow world, where it's nearly impossible to break out of poverty and disillusionment without considerable resources. Education is expensive, but it's the only key to change, improving hearts as well as minds. So we must teach our children well. Teach them to value every human being. Correct them when they mock someone of a different color or race or persuasion. In fact, we must teach generosity: giving it all away. We must teach kindness, gentleness, and ferocity as well: a willingness to stand up to evil, which is what arises when a movement becomes enthralled by violence as a way of getting rid of those who don't agree with them. The culprits might call themselves ISIS, neo-Nazis, the Red Brigades, the Ku Klux Klan, or any number of less extreme-sounding names. Forms of tyranny abound, even in our midst and hiding in plain sight; it requires alertness and courage to resist the persuasions of the media and those who want to convince us that the grave problems in our society lie not within ourselves but with others: immigrants, foreigners, people with alien ideologies, all of those "not like us."

The Way of Jesus teaches the truth that everyone is us. We are the world we seek, and our project, this work designed to further God's gradually realizing kingdom, is first of all within us. But it's also, by extension, the work around us, as we join with others to build this eternal city, taking our stewardship of this planet and our responsibilities for our neighbors seriously. In following this Way, we slowly come to understand that we serve God mainly by meeting and serving those around us, by finding opportunities to love our neighbors. This means listening to them, whatever their political persuasion, whatever their perceived faults, however much they resist our love. And we have to resist the urge to judge them.

"Judging others makes us blind," wrote the great Dietrich Bonhoeffer, not long before he was executed by the Nazis.

I often return to *The Cost of Discipleship* (1937), Bonhoeffer's bracing study of Christian living. In this book, he made a distinction between "cheap grace" and "costly grace," and I am myself trying—*trying*—to seek the latter. Cheap grace is "the preaching of forgiveness without requiring repentance," and it is "grace without discipleship, grace without the cross, grace without Jesus Christ living and incarnate."[1] On the other hand, we have "costly grace," which is "the treasure hidden in the field." This kind of grace invites us to empty ourselves of ourselves, to let go of our petty concerns, to "pluck out the eye" that causes us to stumble, and to leave our fishing nets behind as Jesus's original disciples did, and to follow him wherever he leads us.

This sounds daunting, the idea of taking up the cross and following the Way of Jesus, which is sometimes awkward and requires a great deal of conscious effort, including prayer, observance, discipline, thought, and action. But Christ himself reassured his disciples so beautifully and lovingly in Matthew 11:29 about the benefits that awaited them. This seems a fitting place to end this book, with his pledge to us all: "Come to me, any of you who feel weary and overburdened, and I will promise you rest. Take my yoke upon you and learn from me, for I am gentle and humble in heart, and you will find rest for your souls."

ACKNOWLEDGMENTS

I'm grateful to any number of friends for their help over the years in thinking about *The Way of Jesus*, but I would like to single out Addison Hall, Stan Baker, and Larry Yarborough in particular. Their friendship and conversation have meant so much to me in my thinking about the topics covered in this book. Over the years I have also benefited from intense and inspiring conversations about the meaning of faith in our time with A. N. Wilson. I'm also grateful to my wife, Devon Jersild, for her daily and loving conversations for nearly forty years. Her grace, depth of knowledge, and sympathetic responses cannot possibly be acknowledged enough, ever. I should single out three authors who have challenged and inspired me in recent years: Rowan Williams, Richard Rohr, and Cynthia Bourgeault. My work builds on theirs.

I'm also grateful to Amy Caldwell and Will Myers, my editors at Beacon, who have been meticulous readers, and to Charles Baker, a friend, who has read this manuscript closely and offered suggestions.

My reflections on the Sermon on the Mount appeared, in an earlier version, in *The Good Book: Writers Reflect on Favorite Bible Passages*, edited by Andrew Blauner. I am grateful to Andrew for inviting me to think about this passage in Matthew's Gospel in depth.

NOTES

ONE: JOURNEYING BY FAITH

1. Paul Tillich, *Systematic Theology*, vol. 1 (Chicago: University of Chicago Press, 1951), 236.

2. Rudolf Otto, *The Idea of the Holy*, trans. John W. Harvey (London: Oxford University Press, 1923), 59.

3. This is from the Ronald Gregor Smith translation of 1937, which I prefer to the Walter Kaufmann translation of 1970.

4. Karl Barth, *The Epistle to the Romans*, 6th ed., trans. Edwyn C. Hoskyns (Oxford, UK: Oxford University, 1968), 330–31.

5. From the Smith translation of 1937.

6. Anselm of Canterbury, *Proslogion*, trans. M. J. Charlesworth, *The Major Works* (Oxford, UK: Oxford University Press, 1998), 87.

7. *The Ten Principal Upanishads*, trans. Shree Purohit Swami and W. B. Yeats (London: Faber, 1937), 135.

8. Joseph Campbell, *The Masks of God: Creative Mythology* (New York: Viking, 1968), 678.

9. Norman O. Brown, *Life Against Death: The Psychoanalytical Meaning of History* (Middletown, CT: Wesleyan University Press, 1959), 322.

10. C. S. Lewis, *Mere Christianity* (London: Fount, 1997), 21.

11. Hans Urs von Balthasar, *Prayer*, trans. Graham Harrison (San Francisco: Ignatius Press, 1986), 77.

TWO: THE CHRISTIAN MIND

1. Charles Taylor, *A Secular Age* (Cambridge, MA: Harvard University Press, 2007), 768.

2. Herbert Marcuse, *Eros and Civilization: A Philosophical Inquiry into Freud* (Boston: Beacon Press, 1966), 47.

3. Thomas Merton, *A Search for Solitude: Pursuing the Monk's True Life; the Journals of Thomas Merton, Volume 3: 1952–1960* (San Francisco: HarperOne, 1997), 211.

4. Karl Barth, *Dogmatics in Outline*, trans. G. T. Thompson (New York: Harper, 1959), 154.

5. Anselm of Canterbury, *Proslogion*, 87.

6. Charles Taylor, *Sources of the Self: The Making of the Modern Identity* (Cambridge, MA: Harvard University Press, 1989).

7. Charles Taylor, *Philosophical Arguments* (Cambridge, MA: Harvard University Press, 1995), and *A Secular Age*.

8. Taylor, *A Secular Age*, 60.

9. Taylor, *Philosophical Arguments*, 10.

10. Norman O. Brown, *Love's Body* (New York: Random House, 1966), 257.

11. For a useful and extended discussion of Nietzsche's views on subjectivity, see Andrew Bowie, *Aesthetics and Subjectivity from Kant to Nietzsche* (Manchester, UK: Manchester University Press, 2003).

12. Hans-Georg Gadamer, *Truth and Method* (1975; London: Bloomsbury, 2004), 554.

13. Rowan Williams, *Where God Happens: Discovering Christ in One Another* (Boston: Shambhala Publications, 2005), 12.

14. Taylor, *A Secular Age*, 717–18.

15. See Rosemary Radford Ruether, *Goddesses and the Divine Feminine: A Western Religious History* (Berkeley: University of California Press, 2006).

16. See David Chalmers, "Facing Up to the Problem of Consciousness," *Journal of Consciousness Studies* 2 (1995): 200–219.

17. Thomas Mann, "Freud and the Future," *Daedalus* (Spring 1959): 374.

18. Friedrich Nietzsche, *Human, All-Too-Human*, trans. Helen Zimmern (London: Unwin, 1924), 24.

19. Timothy H. Lim, *The Formation of the Jewish Canon* (New Haven, CT: Yale University Press, 2013), 16.

20. Douglas A. Campbell, *The Deliverance of God: An Apocalyptic Rereading of Justification in Paul* (Grand Rapids, MI: William B. Eerdmans, 2009).

21. Benjamin Wadsworth, *Christian Advice to the Sick and the Well* (Boston: J. Allen, 1714; Early American Imprints, First Series, no. 1720, 1985), 6.

22. Thomas à Kempis, *The Imitation of Christ*, trans. Aloysius Croft and Harold Bolton (Mineola, NY: Dover, 2003), 1.

23. Brown, *Love's Body*, 201.

24. Rowan Williams, *The Wound of Knowledge: Christian Spirituality from the New Testament to St. John of the Cross* (London: Darton, Longman & Todd, 1990), 8.

25. Gadamer, *Truth and Method*, 554.

THREE: THE CHURCH YEAR

1. Joseph Campbell, *The Masks of God: Occidental Mythology* (New York: Viking, 1964), 336.

2. From Richard Rohr's daily blog from the Center for Action and Contemplation, May 31, 2017.

3. C. G. Jung, "Marriage as a Psychological Relationship" (1925), in *Collected Works of C. G. Jung*, vol. 17, trans. G. Adler and R. F. C. Hull (Princeton, NJ: Princeton University Press, 1934), 338.

4. Thomas Merton, *Spiritual Master: The Essential Writings*, ed. Lawrence S. Cunningham (Mahwah, NJ: Paulist Press, 1992), 144.

5. Augustine, "On Nature and Grace," in *Nicene and Post-Nicene Fathers: First Series*, vol. 5, ed. Philip Schaff (New York: Cosimo Classics, 2007), 149.

6. John Calvin, *Institutes of the Christian Religion*, ed. John T. McNeill (Louisville, KY: Westminster John Knox Press, 1960), 746.

7. Quoted in John W. De Gruchy, *Reconciliation: Restoring Justice* (Minneapolis, MN: Augsburg Fortress, 2002), 109.

8. Harvey Cox, *The Future of Faith* (New York: HarperCollins, 2009), 58.

9. Pierre Teilhard de Chardin, *Christianity and Evolution: Reflections on Science and Religion*, trans. René Hague (New York: Harcourt, 2002), 198.

10. Oscar Romero, *The Violence of Love*, trans. James R. Brockman, SJ (Farmington, PA: Bruderhof Foundation, 2003), 25.

11. W. H. Auden, *A Certain World: A Commonplace Book* (New York: Random House, 1970), 168.

12. Augustine, *De Trinitate* 1.3.5.

13. Brown, *Love's Body*, 174.

FOUR: HOW TO BE A CHRISTIAN

1. See the discussion of John Scotus Eriugena—a ninth-century Irish theologian and Neoplatonic poet—in Rik van Nieuwenhove, *An Introduction to Medieval Theology* (Cambridge, UK: Cambridge University Press, 2012).

2. Pew Research Center, *U.S. Public Becoming Less Religious* (Washington, DC: November 3, 2015).

3. Martin Robbins, "Do Four out of Five People Really Believe in Prayer?," *Guardian*, March 26, 2013.

4. Balthasar, *Prayer*, 82.

5. Ibid., 15.

6. *The Heart of Thoreau's Journals*, ed. Odell Shepard (Boston: Houghton Mifflin, 1927), 44.

7. Audre Lorde, *Sister Outsider: Essays and Speeches* (Freedom, CA: Crossing Paths, 1984), 39.

8. *Thoughts for Meditation: A Way to Recovery from Within*, ed. N. Gangulee, preface by T. S. Eliot (London: Faber, 1951), 11.

9. T. S. Eliot, "Religion Without Humanism," in Norman Foerster, ed., *Humanism in America: Essays on the Outlook of Modern Civilization* (New York: Farrar & Rinehart, 1930), 106.

10. Editorial preface in the *Criterion* (April 1932): 467.

11. T. S Eliot, "A Commentary: That Poetry Is Made with Words," *New English Weekly* (April 27, 1939): 27–28.

12. Wendell Berry, *The Art of the Commonplace: The Agrarian Essays* (Berkeley, CA: Counterpoint, 2002), 189.

13. See Jill Jacobs, "The History of 'Tikkun Olam,'" Zeek.net, June 2007.

CONCLUSION

1. Dietrich Bonhoeffer, *The Cost of Discipleship*, trans. Reginald H. Fuller (1937; New York: Macmillan, 1953), 44–45.

INDEX

abortion, 180–81
action (in Christian practice), 175–83
Advent to Christmas period, 110–23; Advent, 110, 115–17; Christmas, importance of, 112; Epiphany, 120–23; Jesus, Gospels on origins of, 112–14; *logos* and, 117–18; magi and, 119–20; Mary and, 114–15; Virgin Birth, 110–11, 114
alienation, 38–39, 55–56
Anselm, Saint, 16–17, 45
Ascension, 138–39
Ash Wednesday, 124
atheism, 46–47, 51–52
Auden, W. H., 24–25, 75, 121, 134, 165
Augustine, Saint, 1, 64, 125, 140
Ave (Hail Mary), 158–59

Balthasar, Hans Urs von, 28, 44, 107, 146, 152–54

Barth, Karl, 13, 14–15, 34, 44
Beatitudes, 92–94
being a Christian, 146–83; action, 175–83; creative thought, 171–75; discipline, 166–71; introduction to, 146–52; observance, 162–66; prayer, 152–62
Bible: context in, importance of, 94; importance of reading of, 174–75; question of infallibility of, 77–78. *See also* New Testament; Old Testament; *specific books of the Bible*
blood, of Jesus, 58
Bodhisattvas, 19
bodies, souls vs., 106
body of Christ, 165
Bright Week (Easter Week, Pascha Week), 138
Brown, Norman O., 21, 47, 102, 103, 143
Buddhism, 19, 20, 82–83, 99, 175–76

Campbell, Joseph, 20–21, 110–11
Cana, miracle at, 56–59
Centering Prayer, 27–28, 160–62
Christ: Christ-mind, 161; Cosmic
    Christ, 114; Jesus and revela-
    tion of, 15; Jesus vs., 131; as
    logos, 117. *See also* Jesus
Christianity: faith community in,
    48–50; goal of, 102; as incar-
    nation religion, 105; prob-
    lematic history of, 35; value
    of, 41–42. *See also* being a
    Christian; Church Year
Christian mind, 34–108; death
    and, 88–92; myths and mir-
    acles, 50–64; religion, descrip-
    tion of, 34–50; Resurrection
    Thinking, 102–8; sacred
    texts, 64–78; Sermon on the
    Mount, 92–101; sin and,
    85–88; suffering and, 79–85.
    See also being a Christian
Christmas, 112–20; date of, 116;
    double versions of, 112–14;
    importance of, 112; *logos*
    and, 117–18; magi, com-
    ing of, 119–20; Mary and,
    114–15. *See also* Advent to
    Christmas period
Christ the King Sunday, 144
Church Year, 109–45; introduc-
    tion to, 109–10; Advent to
    Christmas period, 110–23;
    Lent, 123–29; Easter Tri-
    duum, 130–38; the fifty days,

138–39; Ordinary Time,
    142–45; Pentecost, 139–42
circles, time and, 111
community: epiphanies of, 123;
    faith communities, 48–50,
    107; importance of, 165;
    prayer and, 170–71; religion
    and, 41, 48; Resurrection
    and, 137; Thoreau on, 127;
    Tillich on, 24
concordia scripturarum, 103–4
confession, 124–25, 127–28
Cosmic Christ, 114
creative thought (in Christian
    practice), 171–75
cross, symbolism of, 80, 133

death, 63, 88–92, 135
discernment, 182–83
discipline (in Christian practice),
    166–71
divine spirit, 141
"Do Lord Remember" (Parini),
    31–33
"The Dry Salvages" (Eliot),
    147–49

"East Coker" (Eliot), 135, 147,
    167, 172
Easter (Paschal) Triduum, 129,
    130–38
Easter Week (Bright Week,
    Pascha Week), 138
Eliot, T. S.: on balance, 126;
    on Christian living, 183;

on death, 135; discipline and,
    167–68; on distractions, 166;
    faith choice of, 146–47, 165;
    Four Quartets, 147–49; on
    logos, 117; on poetry, 168; on
    thought and feeling, 171; on
    time, 47, 78–79, 105, 150–52;
    tongues of flames, mention of,
    141–42
Emerson, Ralph Waldo, 1, 2, 37,
    74, 90, 101
enlightenment, 29, 167
environment, stewardship of,
    181–82
Epiphany, 120–23
ethic of reciprocity (Golden
    Rule), 19, 95, 100
evil, 87, 89, 96–97, 156

faith (trust), 2, 16–17, 26, 44, 45,
    107, 173
faith communities, 48–50, 107
Feast of the Transfiguration, 143
the fifty days, 138–39
Four Quartets (Eliot), 147–49,
    165, 167, 183
Francis, Pope, 181–82

glorified body, 57, 91, 137,
    143–44
God: Barth on existence of,
    15; elements comprising,
    54; inner presence of, 145;
    nature of, 1, 40, 104; as one's
    ultimate concern, 12; resting

in God, 25–26; Tillich on, 24;
    time and, 75; in the Trinity,
    154; as vengeful, 140; ways of
    serving, 186
Golden Rule (ethic of reciproc-
    ity), 19, 95, 100
Good Friday, 132–34
Gospels: description of, 71–75;
    mythic moments in, 55;
    nature of, 16, 92. *See also
    individual Gospels*
grace, 125–26, 186

Hail Mary (Ave), 158–59
Harrowing of Hell, 134
Hebrew scriptures (Old Testa-
    ment), 65–70
Hinduism, 20, 150
Holy Saturday, 134–35
holy silence, 153
Holy Spirit, 140–41, 155
Holy Week, 128–29

"I am" statements, 62, 74
Incarnation, 105–6, 110, 112,
    117, 118

James (apostle), on the Law, 164
Jesus: blood of, 58; Christ vs.,
    131; and Christ, revelation of,
    15; core teachings of, 92–101;
    Gospels on origins of, 112–14;
    on the Law, 163–64; on
    love, 49; miracles by, 56–63;
    Ordinary Time for, 121;

prayer and, 153; on right actions, 182; role in the Trinity, 154–55; story of, as *mythos*, 56
Jesus, characterizations of: as embodiment of suffering, 29–30; as incarnation, 105–6, 110, 112, 117, 118; as outsider, 118; as pathway to God, 41–42; as redeemer, 81–82; as son of God, 131; as teacher, 92, 95, 101
Jesus Prayer, 157–58
Jesus: The Human Face of God (Parini), 30–31
Jews. *See* Judaism
John, Gospel of, 16, 61, 72, 74–75, 136
Judaism, 94, 163–65, 176

karma, 18, 94–95, 176
Kierkegaard, Søren, 146, 162
the kingdom, 95
Kingdom of God, 104, 137, 160

language, fall of man and, 47
the Law, 163–65
Lazarus (biblical), 61–63
lectio divina, 169
Lent, 123–29
letting go, 40–43, 83, 156
Lewis, C. S., 23, 80, 109
liberation theology, 179–80
liturgical seasons. *See* Church Year
logos, 74, 107, 117–18, 172
Lord's Prayer, 98, 99, 155–57

love, 36–38, 40, 49, 133
Luke, Gospel of, 16, 72, 73, 113–14
Luther, Martin, 76–77

magi, 119–20
"Magi" (Parini), 119–20
Mark, Gospel of, 16, 72–73
marriage, as discipline, 170
Mary (mother of Jesus), 114–15, 139–40, 149–50
Matthew, Gospel of, 16, 72, 73, 92–101, 112–13
Maundy Thursday, 130, 131–32
Merton, Thomas, 41, 123, 138
"The Miner's Wake" (Parini), 79–80
myths and miracles, 50–64

New Covenant, 97, 102–3
New Testament: discussion of, 70–75; importance of knowledge of, 174. *See also specific books, e.g.,* Luke, Gospel of

observance (in Christian practice), 162–66
Old Testament (Hebrew scriptures), 65–70. *See also specific books, e.g.,* Psalms
Ordinary Time, 142–45
Original Sin, 82

pain. *See* suffering
Palestine, Greek conquering of, 69

Parini, Jay: Auden and, 24–25; churchgoing by, 27; college years, 11–17; contemplative traditions and, 27–28; "Do Lord Remember," 31–33; early years, 2–4; Eastern religions, study of, 17–20; faith journey of, 1–33; father, relationship with, 4–6, 16–17, 129, 174; God, early questioning of, 8–9; in graduate school, 22–26; high school years, 9–11; interests, 6–7, 13–14, 20–21, 26; *Jesus: The Human Face of God*, 30–31; "The Miner's Wake," 79–80; in New Hampshire and Vermont, 26–27; politics and, 122; prayer and, 28; suffering, experiences of, 7–8, 79; Virgin Mary, relationship with, 149–50; writers read by, 28–29, 30, 46, 175
Paschal (Easter) Triduum, 130–38
Pascha Week (Easter Week, Bright Week), 138
Passion of Christ, 80–81, 129
Paul, Saint: Christmas, lack of knowledge of, 112; on discipline, 170; on imperfect vision, 39; on Jewish law, observance of, 164; on learning, 175; letters of, 70–72; on love, 36; on mind of Christ, 44; on the Resurrection,

90–91; on rewards, 18; on self-sacrifice, 43; on transformations, 105–6; on unity with God, 1
Pentecost, 139–42
people of the book. *See* sacred texts
Peter (apostle), 60, 141, 164
poetry, 54, 166. *See also* Eliot, T. S.
prayer, 152–62; author's relationship with, 28–29; Balthasar on, 152–53, 154; Centering Prayer, 160–62; discipline and, 170–71; Lord's Prayer, 155–57; prayer beads, 157; prayer ropes, 157; rosary and, 157–60
Psalms, 67–68, 122
punishment, sin and, 86–87

Reality/reality, 52, 150, 151
reciprocity, principal of, 19, 95, 100
Reformation, 76–77, 125
religion(s): description of, 34–50; importance of knowledge of, 173–74; as term, derivation of, 42. *See also specific religions*
repentance, 126
resting in God, 25–26
Resurrection/resurrection, 44–45, 56, 90–91, 106–7, 136–38
Resurrection Thinking, 102–8, 128

revelation, 45–46, 74
right action (in Christian practice), 175–83
rosaries, 157–60

Sacred Sabbath (Holy Saturday), 134–35
sacred texts, 64–78; final canon of, 76; Hebrew scriptures, 65–70; introduction to, 64–65; New Testament, 70–75; Sola Scriptura, 76–78
sacrifices, 42–43, 81–82
salvation. See enlightenment
Satan, 87. See also evil
secularism, 35–36, 48
self-sacrifice, 43–45
Sermon on the Mount, 92–101, 176, 181
silence: as God's presence, 127, 145, 162; holy silence, 153; prayer and, 160; in Taoism, 17; Thoreau on, 161–62
sin, 85–88
Sola Scriptura, 76–78
soteria, 49
souls, bodies vs., 106
Stations of the Cross, 128–29
stillness, 172
suffering, 7–8, 19, 29–30, 79–88

taking up the Cross, 44
Taylor, Charles, 37, 46, 47, 52, 53
Thomas Aquinas, Saint, 143, 183

Thoreau, Henry David, 109, 127, 161–62
thought, creative (in Christian practice), 171–75
tikkun olam (repair the world), 176
Tillich, Paul, 12–13, 23, 24
time: Auden on, 25; Bergson on, 150; circles and, 111; death and, 90; Eliot's understanding of, 150–52; God as outside of, 75; Incarnation and, 105; Jesus and, 42; nature of, 25–26; rivers as, 78–79
transformation, in Way of Jesus, 44, 63
Triduum (Easter Triduum), 129, 130–38
the Trinity, 140, 154–55
trust (faith), 2, 16–17, 26, 44, 45, 107, 173

Veneration of the Cross, 133
Virgin Birth, 110–11, 114
Virgin Mary, 114–15, 139–40, 149–50
Vulgate, 69–70

Way of Jesus: being a Christian, 146–83; Christian mind, 34–108; Church Year, 109–45; components of, 143, 149; conclusions on, 184–87; Parini, Jay, faith journey of, 1–33; social justice as main goal of, 175